icons

G000036977

2

A Religious Education Programme for 11–14

Mary Jo Martin, RSHM

Anne White

Ann Brook

Paul Gray

Yvonne May

Damian Walmsley

Teacher's Resources

Published by HarperCollins*Publishers* Ltd
77–85 Fulham Palace Road, London W6 8JB

© Department for Catholic Education and Formation, Bishops' Conference of England and Wales

www.**Collins**Education.com
On-line support for schools and colleges

First published 2001

ISBN 0 00 322136 9

Nihil Obstat Fr Anton Cowan, *censor*

Imprimatur Mgr Thomas Egan, V.G.

Westminster, 29th June 2000

British Library Cataloguing in Publication Data
A catalogue record for this book is available from the British Library

Commissioned by Thomas Allain-Chapman

Project management by Kate Haywood and Terry Vittachi

Design and layout by Jordan Publishing Design, Salisbury and Ken Vail Graphic Design, Cambridge

Cover Design by Ken Vail Graphic Design, Cambridge

Cover photograph © Christie's Images Ltd 2000

Printed and bound by Martins the Printers, Berwick-upon-Tweed

LIVING
Catholic Bishops' Conference of England & Wales
Sharing
OUR FAITH
a national project of catechesis & religious education

Collins

Foreword

On behalf of the Bishops' Conference, I am very pleased to welcome the publication of *Icons*.

Diocesan RE advisers, teachers and many others from all the dioceses of England and Wales have worked extremely hard in the production of this programme, which forms an important part of the National Project. On behalf of the Bishops' Conference, I thank them for their dedication and perseverance.

At the Low Week 2000 Meeting of the Bishops' Conference of England and Wales, the bishops published a statement on Religious Education in Catholic Schools. In it they said that the primary purpose of classroom religious education in a Catholic school is:

'To draw pupils into a systematic study of the teaching of the Church, the saving mystery of Christ which the Church proclaims.' (para 7)

In undertaking this task, schools will benefit greatly from the provision of good teaching resources. For this reason I welcome *Icons*, for it will help Catholic schools to fulfil these expectations during the critical years of Key Stage Three.

In their statement, the bishops also stated:

'The importance of the teacher of RE cannot be exaggerated. We are most grateful to all those teachers who, week in and week out, have contributed to the religious education of pupils in our schools. We salute the generosity of the teachers who have brought not only a love of their faith to their teaching but also a deep concern for the well-being of every pupil.' (para 12)

I gladly repeat that thanks and express my own encouragement for teachers in their important task.

† Vincent Nichols
Archbishop of Birmingham
Chairman
Department of Catholic Education and Formation
6 June 2000

Acknowledgements

The publishers gratefully acknowledge the following for permission to reproduce copyright material. Every effort has been made to trace copyright holders, but in some cases this has proved impossible. The publishers would be happy to hear from any copyright holder that has not been acknowledged. Any omission will be corrected at the very first opportunity.

Extract from *A History of the English Church and People* by Bede, translated by Leo Sherley-Price (Penguin Classics 1955, Revised edition 1968), © Leo Shirley-Price 1955, 1968; reprinted with permission of Penguin Books Limited.

Excerpts from the English translation of *Rite of Confirmation, 2nd Edition*, © 1975, International Committee of English in the Liturgy Inc (ICEL); excerpts from the English translation of *Rite of Penance* © 1974, ICEL; excerpts from the English translation of *Pastoral Care of the Sick* © 1982, ICEL; all rights reserved; reprinted with permission.

Illustrations
Nigel Jordan pp. 46,
Alyson MacNeill pp. 48, 50
Tony Forbes pp. 52, 58, 59
Terry Riley p. 60

Religious Education in Catholic Schools

At their Low Week Conference, May 2000, the Catholic Bishops of England and Wales approved the statement *Religious Education in Catholic Schools*. It is 'the fruit of a long period of discussion, public consultation and the symposium on classroom RE which was held in January 2000'. From the statement:

In the life of the Catholic school, religious education plays a central and vital part. At the heart of Catholic education lies the Christian vision of the human person. This vision is expressed and explored in religious education. Therefore, religious education is never simply one subject among many, but the foundation of the entire educational process. The beliefs and values studied in Catholic religious education inspire and draw together every aspect of the life of a Catholic school. We are committed to classroom RE, then, because all pupils have the right to receive an overall education which will enable them, in the light of the faith of the Church, to engage with the deepest questions of life and find reasons for the hope which is within them (1 Peter 3:15). Religious education is, then, the core subject in a Catholic school.

In 1996, we published the *Religious Education Curriculum Directory for Catholic Schools*. This stated clearly the overall aims of classroom RE and its more precise objectives. They can be summarised as stating that religious education in a Catholic school is a comprehensive and systematic study of the mystery of God, of the life and teachings of Jesus Christ, the teachings of his Church, the central beliefs that Catholics hold, the basis for them and the relationship between faith and life; in a manner which encourages investigation and reflection by the pupils, develops the appropriate skills and attitudes, and promotes free, informed and full response to God's call in everyday life. In the words of the *Curriculum Directory*, the outcome of Catholic religious education 'is religiously literate young people who have the knowledge, understanding and skills – appropriate to their age and capacity – to think spiritually, ethically and theologically, and who are aware of the demands of religious commitment in everyday life' (p. 10).

> 'A Catholic school which promotes the best possible teaching of religious education is fulfilling its true purpose.'
>
> From the Bishops' Statement

The specific contribution to the life of the Catholic school of classroom RE is primarily educational, for its primary purpose is to draw pupils into a systematic study of the teachings of the Church, the saving mystery of Christ which the Church proclaims. Excellence in religious education, then, will be characterised by a clarity of succinct religious learning objectives and of key content, by appropriate methodologies, rigour, richness of resources, achievement of identified outcomes and accurate methods of assessment. Classroom RE will be a challenging educational engagement between the pupil, the teacher and the authentic subject material.

RE teaching in a Catholic school will be enlightened by the faith of the school community and by the faith of the RE teacher. Its educational focus will be formed and enhanced by the vitality of faith. For some in the classroom, religious education may well be received as catechesis, deepening and enhancing their personal faith; for some it will be evangelisation, the first time they will have been presented, personally, with the truths of living faith. Nevertheless, its primary purpose is the step by step study of the mystery of Christ, the teaching of the Church and its application in daily life. The criteria by which it is to be judged are educational.

When classroom RE displays these educational characteristics, then its specific contribution to the life of the Catholic school, which as a whole is a catechetical community, becomes apparent. Then the complementarity of the various roles which contribute to the life of the school is also clarified: the role of the leadership of the school as a catechetical community, the role of the chaplaincy of the school, and the partnership in the religious life of the pupils between the school, the parishes and the families. All these have a part to play in the handing on of faith and its expression and exploration in daily life.

Welcome to Icons

Icons is prepared for Catholic schools in England and Wales at the request of the Bishops' Conference, to implement its *Religious Education Curriculum Directory* (*RECD*, 1996).

The *Catechism of the Catholic Church* is the source and foundation for the *Curriculum Directory* and for *Icons*. Throughout the teacher's notes cross references to the *Catechism* are provided and relevant paragraphs are included in 'For Reflection'. In addition, in each section of work the key doctrinal content is given from the *Catetchism* text.

Icons offers a systematic programme, practical help for classroom teaching and the essential background needed to develop and expand the material to fit the particular needs of different schools and students. It is important for the delivery of curriculum religious education that the principles and vision of the programme are appreciated.

It is out of a shared **VISION** of religious education

that **RESPONSIBILITIES** are identified,

the **PROCESS** is understood and developed

and the most relevant **RESOURCES** are selected and used effectively (see p. 5).

What's in a name?

Icons have a long tradition in Christian art, and are more than art.

They are 'windows into heaven'; 'gateways' for God and to God.

Icons are a profession of faith in the holiness of God the Creator and creation as God's work. (*CCC* 339)

Icons are a profession of faith in the Incarnation. The Word was 'made flesh and came to live among us' (John 1:14). In the human face of Jesus 'we see our God made visible and so are caught up in love of the God we cannot see.' (*CCC* 477–8)

Icons are a profession of faith in Christian belief in God, for whom creation and human life are means of communication and places of encounter. (*CCC* 31–5)

For these reasons, iconographers use only natural materials and prepare for their task with prayer.

In the language of computers also, an 'icon' is a gateway, and the word has come to have a further meaning in speaking of a person who is a role model. The *Catechism* uses it in this sense, describing Mary as 'Icon of the Church' (*CCC* 972), and the ordained minister as an 'icon' of Christ the priest. Speaking of the Christian name that is given to each person in Baptism, the *Catechism* says: 'God calls each one by name. Everyone's name is sacred. The name is the icon of the person. It demands respect as a sign of the dignity of the one who bears it.' (*CCC* 2158)

In all this, religious education can find inspiration. It is a reminder that religious education is about more than the imparting of knowledge. Teachers and students 'open gateways and windows' for one another in the discovery of the gospel that 'speaks' for all time. The dignity of teacher and student is affirmed in recognising that the world and the human person are points of departure for knowing God. (*CCC* 31)

Created in God's image and called to love and know him, the person who seeks God discovers certain ways of coming to know him. These are also called proofs for the existence of God, not in the sense of proofs in the natural sciences, but rather in the sense of 'converging and convincing arguments' which allow us to attain certainty about the truth.

These 'ways' of approaching God from creation have a twofold point of departure: the physical world, and the human person. (*CCC* 31)

Vision

Presents the structure
of the programme for Years 7, 8 and 9.
(pp. 4–10)

Responsibilities

sets religious education
within the wider context of
the Church's teaching tradition and
looks at different roles in the religious
development of students. Clarity about
their role in the classroom enables
teachers to select the resources
that will engage them and
their students in the process
to best effect.
(p. 11)

Process

describes the threefold
process for religious education in
Icons – Research, Revelation,
Response – and its practical
implementation.
(pp. 12–15)

**Scheme of
work and resources**

identifies content to be
taught and provides resources:
Learning outcomes
Teaching and learning process
Foundations in key stages 1 and 2
Links to RE Curriculum Directory
Tips for teachers
For reflection
Copymasters
(pp. 16–62)

Icons: the programme

Icons offers a structured, progressive and developmental programme for Years 7, 8 and 9. The structure is shaped by the questions about *Identity*, *Purpose* and *Fulfilment* which the *Catechism* states concern the foundations of human and Christian life. (*CCC* 282)

These questions are addressed and explored in the light of Christian faith in **Jesus Christ**, the **human person**, the **Church** and the ways faith is celebrated, lived and prayed through the **sacraments** and the **liturgical year**.

There are three units for each year. Each includes all the five components: Jesus Christ, the Church, the human person, the sacraments and the liturgical year.

The first and major part of the work of each unit (A) directs the rest of the term's work (B,C,D,E). *Icons* provides for a three term year in which terms two and three vary in length. A flexible component (2/3E) is provided to accommodate this variation.

For each year material for a study of one major world faith is included. This can be studied either as a distinct component or integrated into the year's work.

2 the HUMAN PERSON — called to fullness of life

3 the CHURCH — its life and mission

I the life and teaching of JESUS CHRIST

5 Catholic belief and life: LITURGICAL YEAR

4 Catholic belief and life: SACRAMENTS

Year 8

Unit 1	LIFE TIMES – Jesus Christ: icon for all times (Identity)	
1A	**In a time and place**	*Jesus Christ*
1B	Making history	*Church*
1C	A sense of vocation	*Human person*
1D	A lifetime's work	*Sacraments*
1E	Future forward	*Liturgical year*

Unit 2	LIVING HISTORY – Church: icon of Jesus Christ (Purpose)	
2A	**The People of God**	*Church*
2B	In search of wholeness	*Sacraments*
2C	Saviour of the world	*Jesus Christ*
2D	People of spirit and truth	*The human person*
2/3E	Churches together	*Liturgical year/Church*
	Judaism	*Other faiths*

Unit 3	HERE IN THIS PLACE – human person: icon of God the Saviour (Fulfilment)	
3A	**A place for everyone**	*Human person*
3B	A sacred place	*Sacraments*
3C	A place for hopes and dreams	*Jesus Christ*
3D	A place for saints	*Liturgical year*

Year 7

Unit 1	THE LIVING CHURCH – Church: icon of community (Identity)	
1A	**About belonging**	*Church*
1B	A matter of identity	*Jesus Christ*
1C	Living relationships	*Human person*
1D	Celebrating initiation	*Sacraments*
1E	Celebrating Christ's Mass	*Liturgical year*

Unit 2	CHRIST THE LIGHT – Jesus Christ: icon for human life (Purpose)	
2A	**Jesus the Saviour**	*Jesus Christ*
2B	Celebrating Easter	*Liturgical year*
2C	Living as Easter people	*Church*
2D	Called to change	*Sacraments*
2/3E	A place for prayer	*Human person / Jesus Christ*
	Hinduism	*Other faiths*

Unit 3	BECOMING FULLY HUMAN – human person: icon of God the Creator (Fulfilment)	
3A	**Who am I?**	*Human person*
3B	Celebrating Pentecost	*Liturgical year*
3C	Life shared	*Church*
3D	Celebrating life	*Sacraments*

Year 9

Unit 1	FAITH CHALLENGES – human person: icon of God the Spirit (Identity)	
1A	**To be a pilgrim ...**	*Human person*
1B	Time challenges	*Church*
1C	Leadership challenges	*Jesus Christ*
1D	Prayer challenges	*Sacraments*
1E	Hope challenges	*Liturgical year*

Unit 2	AT THE HEART OF BELIEF – Jesus: icon of faith and love of the Father (Purpose)	
2A	**Word made Flesh**	*Jesus Christ*
2B	Love	*Church*
2C	Sacrifice	*Sacraments*
2D	Resurrection	*Liturgical year*
2/3E	Something worth living for	*Human person*
	Islam	*Other faiths*

Unit 3	A VISION FOR LIVING – Church: icon of the Kingdom (Fulfilment)	
3A	**The common good**	*Church*
3B	Living powerful lives	*Liturgical year*
3C	Living commitment	*Sacraments*
3D	Living the Gospel	*Jesus Christ*

The essential role of theological reflection

If the Church's vision of education is to be implemented faithfully, theological reflection is a crucial part of teachers' understanding, preparation and planning. For *Icons*, this must be a Department activity so that everyone, particularly the non-specialist, is clear and confident about what learning and teaching is involved. Material to support theological and educational reflection is offered for all areas of work (*Scheme of work and resources,* pp. 16–45). These pages are indispensable for the successful use of the programme and offer specific help for practical and reflective preparation.

The material that follows invites reflection on the five major components of the programme. Here, as throughout the programme, the selection offered for reflection is not exhaustive. Heads of Department and others may wish to include material from their own resources and other documents of the Church's teaching – CCRS course material is another useful source.

Theology

Catholic faith proclaims belief in God who takes the initiative in relationship, whose Self-Revelation begins with the gift of life, and whose love is personal and unassailable. This love becomes tangible and visible in Jesus Christ and his unique sacrifice. The Son of God came to live and die for sinners, and his death and resurrection bring new life for all. This new life is poured out for the world by the indwelling presence of the Holy Spirit.

Catechism

The Revelation of God in Jesus Christ, 'since it is the new and definitive Covenant, will never pass away; and no new public revelation is to be expected before the glorious manifestation of our Lord Jesus Christ. Yet even if Revelation is already complete, it has not been made completely explicit; it remains for Christian faith gradually to grasp its full significance over the course of the centuries.' (*CCC* 66)

Experience

In the degree of the truth of our conception of [Jesus] our minds grow broader, deeper and warmer; our hearts grow wiser and kinder; our humour deeper and more tender; we become more aware of the wonder of life; our senses become more sensitive; our sympathies stronger; our capacity for giving and receiving greater … (Caryll Houselander, 1901–1954)

Question

Who/what has shaped my notions of God?

Scripture

The Old and New Testaments proclaim faith in God present, loving, guiding and caring for Israel.

But now thus says the Lord … Do not fear, for I have redeemed you; I have called you by name, you are mine. Should you pass through the waters, I shall be with you; or through rivers, they will not swallow you up. Should you walk through fire, you will not suffer, and the flame will not burn you. For I am Yahweh, your God, the Holy One of Israel, your Saviour.

(Isaiah 43:1–3)

Jesus Christ: Revelation, the Trinity

I am with you always; yes, to the end of time.

(Matthew 28:20)

The New Testament reveals Father, Son and Spirit and invites a personal response to Jesus Christ.

God raised this man Jesus to life, and of that we are all witnesses. Now raised to the heights by God's right hand, he has received from the Father the Holy Spirit who was promised, and what you see and hear is the outpouring of that Spirit … For this reason the whole House of Israel can be certain that the Lord and Christ whom God has made is this Jesus whom you crucified.

(Acts 2:32–3, 36)

Who do you say that I am?

(Mark 8:29)

The Creed
*I believe in God the Father almighty, creator of heaven and earth …
I believe in Jesus Christ, his only Son, our Lord …
I believe in the Holy Spirit …*

(from The Apostles' Creed)

Theology

Belief that each one is created in the 'image of God' is the foundation for all that the Church teaches, promotes and defends regarding human dignity, rights, freedom and responsibility. Sin, personal and social, distorts this image. In the Easter Vigil the Church remembers the 'necessary sin of Adam which gained for us so great a redeemer'.

A new creation comes through the Son of God who became human in order that 'human beings might become God' (St Athanasius, AD295–373). By the power of the Holy Spirit, men and women are led to intimacy with God and eternal happiness. This vocation is the root of human need to live in society. It is the basis of moral and social codes of justice and peace and the Christian vocation to love each neighbour as oneself.

Catechism

Catechesis on creation is of major importance. It concerns the very foundation of human and Christian life: for it makes explicit the response of the Christian faith to the basic question that men [and women] of all times have asked themselves: 'Where do we come from?' 'Where are we going?' 'What is our origin?' 'What is our end?' 'Where does everything that exists come from and where is it going?' The two questions, the first about the origin and the second about the end, are inseparable. They are decisive for the meaning and orientation of our life and actions. (*CCC* 282)

Being in the image of God, the human individual possesses the dignity of a *person*, who is not just something, but someone ... (*CCC* 357)

Scripture

The Scriptures proclaim human dignity and destiny.

When I see the heavens, the work of your hands, the moon and the stars which you arranged, what are we that you should keep us in mind, men and women that you care for us? Yet you have made us little less than gods; and crowned us with glory and honour, gave us power over the works of your hands, put all things under our feet.

(Psalms 8:3–7)

And all of us with our unveiled faces like mirrors reflecting the glory of the Lord, are being transformed into the image that we reflect in brighter and brighter glory; this is the working of the Lord who is the Spirit.

(2 Corinthians 3:18)

**2
The
human person**

Creed

I believe in the communion of saints, the resurrection of the body and the life everlasting.

(from the Apostles' Creed)

Experience

The good news is that you really don't know how great you can be, how much you can love, what you can accomplish and what your potential is. How can you top good news like that?

(Anne Frank, 1928–1944)

Question

Who and what has developed or diminished my self-respect? What contribution have I been able to make to the dignity, rights, freedom of others?

Scripture

Scripture proclaims the growth and formation of the Church, seeking to live the gospel, united in worship and celebration, confident in God's forgiveness and mercy.

Each day, with one heart, they went to the Temple, but met in their houses for the breaking of bread; they shared their goods gladly and generously; they praised God and were looked up to by everyone. Day by day the Lord added to their community those destined to be saved.

(Acts 2:44–7)

In him you, also, when you had heard the word of truth, the gospel of your salvation, and had believed in him, were marked with the seal of the promised Holy Spirit; this is the pledge of our inheritance toward redemption as God's own people, to the praise of his glory.

(Ephesians 1:13–4)

Theology

Catholic belief about the Church is rooted in faith in God as Trinity: the Church is the communion of all peoples, called by the Father, united by Christ and empowered by the Holy Spirit to be the sacrament of communion for the world.

Each sacrament brings about a special relationship with God and with the Church. The sacrament of the Eucharist is the fullest expression of communion with Christ in his offering of himself to the Father.

Christ's life, death and resurrection are the reason for all the Church's celebrations, feasts and seasons. In the Church's liturgy God's loving plan of salvation is revealed and communicated. Christian liturgy has, therefore, a dual dimension: a response in faith and love to the divine blessing, and a continual prayer for the outpouring of the Spirit so that the blessings and gifts of God's love may bear fruit.

Catechism

To reunite all his children, scattered and led astray by sin, the Father willed to call the whole of humanity together into his Son's Church. The Church is the place where humanity must rediscover its unity and salvation. The Church is 'the world reconciled' …(*CCC* 845)

In the one family of God. 'For if we continue to love one another and to join in praising the Most Holy Trinity – all of us who are sons of God and form one family in Christ – we will be faithful to the deepest vocation of the Church.' (*CCC* 959)

From the beginning until the end of time the whole of God's work is a *blessing*. From the liturgical poem of the first creation to the canticles of the heavenly Jerusalem, the inspired authors proclaim the plan of salvation as one vast divine blessing. (*CCC* 1079)

The Church which is the Body of Christ participates in the offering of her Head. With him, she herself is offered whole and entire. (*CCC* 1368)

3, 4, 5
The Church —
faith celebrated, lived and prayed through the sacraments and liturgical year

Creed

I believe in …
the holy catholic Church …
the communion of saints,
the forgiveness of sins …

(from The Apostles' Creed)

Experience

The church is never a place, but always a people. The church is you who pray, not where you pray.

(Anon)

Question

What experience do I bring of 'being Church', of praise and worship, of thanksgiving for blessings?

The RE student

Students live in a world full of conflicting values and a society whose prevailing attitude is that religion, religious belief and practice are irrelevant. They bring to RE many of the values and attitudes of this society, of their families and their experience of Church. Students at key stage 3 are in the process of exploring the values, attitudes and qualities that will guide their adult lives. *Icons* addresses issues, questions and concerns that face them today. Learning to ask questions with confidence is an essential part of education. 'The Church's concern is not simply with the teaching of religious truths. Rather it is in the fostering and nourishing of all that makes for a fully human life.' (Cardinal Basil Hume, *Recapturing the Vision*, 1991) In a Catholic school, the presentation of and clarity about the Christian response to questions should never short-circuit discussion. Precisely by presenting clearly that which is true it should lead to the discovery of possibilities and new horizons.

Curriculum religious education is about the multi-cultural, multi-racial Catholic faith and life in today's multi-cultural, multi-faith society. The Catholic Church calls its members to approach other faiths with respect and to recognise in them signs of God's presence (*Nostrae aetate*, 196). This is not an abstract study, but one that aims at enriching students' own spiritual journey. 'Our approach to other faiths is one of "walking on holy ground".' (Vincent Nichols, 'The Church's Mission in Education in a Multi-faith Society' in *Partners in Mission,* CES and *Briefing*, 1997)

RE teachers

The same principles of good teaching apply to RE as to any other subject. *Icons* offers a programme and schemes of work for Ys 7, 8 and 9 that present learning outcomes, clear content and assessment procedures. The Process offers the experienced teacher flexibility and opportunities for creativity. For the inexperienced teacher, it offers a structured approach that will develop confidence about the Church's teaching and how to present it according to the age and capacity of the students. The *Teaching and Learning Process* for each section of work (pp. 16–46) assists selection by outlining the material offered in the student's book. This indicates clearly the Assessment material. It includes notes and cross references to the *Catechism. For reflection* provides material to enable theological reflection to be a key part of departmental preparation. Heads of Department and others will have their own contributions to make to this.

The RE Department

The RE Department, at the heart of the Catholic school, has a twofold role:
◆ to manage the delivery, teaching and learning of religious education in the school through:
  ● clear documentation setting out the vision and direction of RE
  ● regular departmental meetings
  ● planning the RE curriculum to ensure progression and development
  ● offering support and ongoing professional development opportunities for RE teachers
  ● ensuring access to good quality resources and evaluating the quality of teaching and learning in RE
◆ to contribute, in collaboration with the headteacher and school chaplain, to the religious life of the school and students' spiritual and moral development through:
  ● offering support and encouragement to staff for this whole school concern
  ● providing direction, when necessary, for whole school involvement in the spiritual and religious life of the school
  ● offering expertise and support to staff and pupils in areas relating to religious and moral issues.

religious education

engages

facilitates reflection

develops

assesses

encourages

teaches

prepares

informs

measures

challenges

questions

supports

How to use the programme

Icons: the process

The *Catechism* begins with the human search for meaning, the Divine Revelation of God who comes to meet us, and the response of faith. (*CCC* 26)

Religious education is both an 'outward' and 'inward' journey. The former engages students in 'learning *about*'. They acquire knowledge and understanding through study, discussion and reflection. The latter engages students in 'learning *from*'. This leads them into critical reflection on their own experience, appreciation of the Christian story and a dialogue between these two.

The Bishops' *Religious Education Curriculum Directory* presents the curriculum content of religious education. *Icons* is a programme for implementing that content for key stage 3 students. It does this through a three-fold process: **Research, Revelation, Response**. It provides a methodology and structure. It is a teaching and learning process. It engages students in the continuing journey of learning about and learning from the Catholic vision and understanding of life. In this sense, *Icons* aims 'to communicate the rich vision of faith to today's seekers'. (*RECD* p. 6)

The QCA document, *Religious Education Non Statutory Guidance on RE* (QCA/00/576) recognises that there is a variety of starting points and teaching approaches. It describes three teaching and learning approaches: conceptual, ethnographic, human or personal (p. 22). In each it highlights the need to 'identify a key aspect of human or personal experience to create a bridge to the religious concept'.

RESEARCH introduces students to the area of work being studied:

◆ it raises questions about meaning and what is involved in this study

◆ it starts from where students are

◆ it takes aspects of the area of work being studied and links them to students' experience and previous learning

◆ it invites enquiry and reflection on the area of work being studied

◆ it offers glimpses of new horizons

◆ it challenges students to reflect critically on their own experience

◆ it invites and enables students to begin to look at their own experience in the light of the living witness of the Church

◆ it leads students into the second part of the process.

REVELATION leads students into the heart of the area of work being studied:

◆ it deepens their knowledge and understanding of the Word of God as it is welcomed, believed, celebrated, lived and prayed by the Church

◆ it enables them to reflect on the reality of God in everyday experiences

◆ it offers them the authentic richness of the Christian story

◆ it invites, encourages and challenges them to engage in personal dialogue with the Christian message

◆ it challenges them to appreciate the call to faith in Christ

◆ it enables students to understand and appreciate, through study of other faiths, the common human quest for meaning, truth and happiness and God at work in human lives.

Note that the terms **Research, Revelation** and **Response** name the process for teachers. The terms are not used in the students' texts.

In the students' texts Response is named:
  Making connections: Y7
  Links: Y8
  Response: Y9

RESPONSE leads students into consolidation and evaluation of their learning:

◆ it encourages and challenges them to relate faith to life and life to faith

◆ it provides opportunities for assessment, recording and reporting

◆ it engages students in a dialogue between their own experience and the Christian story and Tradition

◆ it offers opportunities for growth and development in learning about and learning from their study

◆ it invites and provides opportunities for reflection on possible action that might follow learning.

Managing time

Classroom RE 'requires the unequivocal support of the management of every Catholic school. It also requires ten percent of the length of the taught week for each Key Stage of education' (Low Week Statement). *Icons* is written to meet this requirement. For each section of work, allow: **Research** one-quarter of the time; **Revelation** one-half of the time; and **Response** one-quarter of the time. The process allows flexibility. Clarity about the learning outcomes and the process will give teachers the confidence to adapt and select material appropriately in order to meet the different needs of students. Depending on the timetable structure for RE teaching, *Icons* can be managed in the following way.

MODEL 1 (3 lessons a week)

Unit 1 approximately 15 weeks

A = 12 lessons	B, C, D, E = 8 lessons each
Research 2/3	Research 2
Revelation 7	Revelation 4
Response 2/3	Response 2

Unit 2 approximately 11 weeks

A = 9 lessons	B, C, D, E = 6 lessons
Research 2	Research 1/2
Revelation 5	Revelation 3/4
Response 2	Response 1

Unit 3 approximately 12 weeks

A = 10 lessons	B, C, D, E = 6 lessons
Research 2/3	Research 1/2
Revelation 5	Revelation 3/4
Response 2/3	Response 1

MODEL 2 (2 lessons a week)

Unit 1 approximately 15 weeks

A = 10 lessons	B, C, D, E = 5 lessons each
Research 2	Research 1
Revelation 6	Revelation 3
Response 2	Response 1

Unit 2 approximately 11 weeks

A = 6 lessons	B, C, D, E = 4 lessons
Research 1/2	Research 1
Revelation 3/4	Revelation 2
Response 1	Response 1

Unit 3 approximately 12 weeks

A = 6 lessons	B, C, D, E = 4 lessons
Research 1/2	Research 1
Revelation 3/4	Revelation 2
Response 1	Response 1

Planning is essential to the successful use of *Icons*.

Long-term planning (staff Inset days)

1. Read through the Units to be studied (year's work).
2. Check the teachers' pages for additional information.
3. Get a sense and understanding of the flow of the material and direction of the work.
4. Identify how Section A gives direction to B, C, D and E in each Unit.
5. Begin to reflect on how you might teach the Units.

Medium-term planning (before the beginning of each term)

1. Read through the Unit to be studied (term's work).
2. Check the teachers' notes for additional information.
3. Plan out the number of lessons for each part of the Unit, keeping in mind the recommended time allocation and the importance of Section A.
4. Identify how Section A gives focus and direction to the rest of the Unit.
5. Identify what additional resources you will need to teach the Unit.

Short-term planning (at the beginning of each term and each week)

1. Prepare lesson plans for Section A and other sections of the Unit.
2. Identify the learning outcomes for each lesson.
3. Select the teaching strategies and student activities you will use to achieve the learning outcomes.
4. Prepare the assignments and tasks you will use in each lesson and the extended tasks that might be useful.
5. Plan your assessment procedure for ensuring the learning outcomes have been achieved.

Five habits of an effective *Icons* teacher

1. Be clear about how each lesson fits into the **section** and **unit** of work.
2. Know how the **process** works.
3. **Time management** for each part of the process is crucial.
4. Share the **learning outcomes** with your students.
5. **Assess** student learning every lesson.

Diagnostic assessment

Y7: *Check out what you know*

Y8: *Check your learning*

Y9: *Think back*

The Level Descriptors for Attainment Targets for Catholic Schools have been prepared by the National Board of Religious Inspectors and Advisors (Rejoice Publications, September 2000)

Assessment in Icons

Assessment lies at the heart of the teaching and learning process. It:

◆ recognises and values the unique contribution of each student's abilities and aptitudes

◆ encourages personal commitment to learning and responsibility for one's own learning

◆ promotes collaborative learning and communication between all involved in a student's education

◆ measures and provides information about a student's progress and mastery of skills.

In *Icons*, all formal assessment tasks are related to the *Revelation* stage of the process.

A whole class **Diagnostic assessment** is provided either at the beginning of each section of work or at the start of the *Revelation* stage. It enables teachers to identify students' previous learning and, if necessary, to make changes to lesson planning based on what students know or do not know, understand or do not understand, can or cannot do.

For each section of work the following are provided:

Formative, class work: differentiated. It provides information about ongoing progress and development which can be shared with all involved in students' learning. Three levels are offered, from which the teacher will choose the appropriate task to suit each learner:

    A. Core: all students will do this

    B. Developed: most students will do this

    C. Extended: some students will do this.

Formative, homework: either a single homework or an extended exercise.

Summative, classwork: *Testing times* (Y7); *Test* (Y8); *Assessment* (Y9).

This assesses AT1 (see below). Formative assessment tasks assess both AT1 and AT2. Alternatively, departments may wish to draw up their own end of study procedure for measuring student learning.

Attainment targets, levels and level descriptors

In *Icons* there are two attainment targets (AT):

AT1: Knowledge and understanding of religion: *learning about* religion; knowledge, understanding, ability to evaluate

AT2: Reflection on meaning: *learning from* religion; ability to reflect on meaning.

The tasks and assessment exercises in *Icons* cover both these targets. Attainment levels and level descriptors to help teachers identify student progress and development are provided (p. 15).

Differentiation in Icons

Icons offers teachers one key differentiated task for each component of work in each unit at three levels: core, developed and extended (See above and relevant pages throughout the *Scheme of work and resources* pp. 16–45)

Recording in Icons

Recording and evaluation assist teachers in both planning and teaching. The end of Unit record sheet (p. 63) may be attached to a student's record. *Icons* recognises the school or RE Department will have a policy for recording.

Reporting in Icons

Reporting provides feedback to students. It also informs teachers, parents, governors and diocesan authorities about the content and quality of religious education within the school. *Icons* recognises that the RE Department will follow the school policy for reporting.

Attainment target level descriptors

From *Attainment Levels for Religious Education in Catholic Schools* (NBRIA, September 2000). Levels 4–7 are given below. Departments will need to have access to the NBRIA document and be aware of Levels 1–3 and 8–10.

Level	AT1: Knowledge and understanding of religion: learning *about* religion	AT2: Reflection on meaning: learning *from* religion
Four	Pupils can explain that beliefs, special buildings, language, places and books are features of religion. They can show how religious practice shapes people's lives. They are able to explain the significance of liturgical actions for believers.	Pupils can discuss beliefs and values which influence behaviour. They can recognise that everyone has personal beliefs and values. They are able to ask questions of meaning arising from their own and others' experience. They can identify places and situations which may be conducive to reflection and prayer.
Five	Pupils can demonstrate that there are different types of religious commitment. They are able to recognise that only human beings are 'religious'. They can use some forms of religious language to convey meaning.	Pupils are able to identify some religious and non-religious beliefs and values different from their own. They are able to show that people have different answers to questions of meaning. They can explain how periods of silence and stillness may be used for reflection and prayer.
Six	Pupils are able to identify some religious principles which others follow. They can select appropriate information to support an argument related to religious issues. They are able to explain some religious concepts and can analyse specific religious practices.	Pupils can give reasons for their own religious or non-religious beliefs and values, and explain their significance. They are able to show that questions of meaning have inspired creative work. They are able to recognise that every person has the capacity to be inspired.
Seven	Pupils are able to explain some of the unifying principles of religion. They can apply religious principles and beliefs to issues of social justice and morality. They are able to show the power of symbols within belief systems. They can differentiate between religious and secular world views.	Pupils are able to explore alternative views and possibilities of commitment, including religious commitment. They can demonstrate the importance of the right to choose, and hold religious and non-religious beliefs and values. They are able to recognise that religions seek answers to questions about human existence. They can explain the importance of reflection.

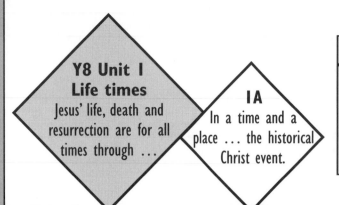

Jesus was born into and raised in the **Jewish faith**. In the synagogue he learned the **Hebrew Scriptures** and joined in the community's prayer; he went to the Temple to worship. The **religion** and **culture** of the time was the context for his life and teaching.

Teaching and learning process: *learning outcomes*

By the end of this section of work, students should:

◆ appreciate the importance of cultural, social and religious background for people's understanding of themselves and others
◆ know and understand that Jesus was born, lived and worked within the Jewish faith community of his time.

At each stage, select activities to fulfil the learning outcomes.

Research

Students will have the opportunity to investigate and reflect upon:

◆ what and how different cultural, social and religious backgrounds contribute to understanding and appreciating oneself and others in class, in school and in society.

Research

◆ *Start where you are* (p. 6): explores the richness and challenge of cultural diversity.
◆ Key words and concepts: *diversity, culture, to cultivate.*
◆ *Pause for thought* (p. 6): link to *Jesus the Jew* (p. 7): use art to explore how cultures claim Jesus. Representations from Cameroon, China and India.
◆ **Diagnostic assessment**: *Check your learning* (p. 7): look for awareness of the historical situation, for example, Palestine, an occupied country; at a crossroads of the Roman empire; its powerful neighbours, Egypt, Persia and Babylon.

Revelation

Students will have the opportunity to learn about and reflect upon:

◆ the Jewish context for the life and mission of Jesus
◆ some of the Jewish beliefs and practices he would have known
◆ the place of the Hebrew Scriptures in Jewish life
◆ some of the different social, cultural and religious groups of Jesus' time.

Revelation

◆ *Jesus' life in Palestine* (pp. 8–11): focuses on:
(a) *The Synagogue* (pp. 8–9) place of prayer and learning; the Torah, the Law; not in a narrow legal sense – for many Jews the study of the Torah will be one of the joys of heaven. In Luke's gospel Jesus announces his mission in the synagogue at Nazareth.
(b) *The Temple* (pp. 10–11) place of worship and sacrifice; roles and privileges in Jewish community; context for gospel passages. The Church reverences the Old Testament as true Word of God (*CCC* 121–123) and directs attention to the richness that comes from knowledge of Jewish faith, life and liturgy. (*CCC* 1096)
◆ *Politics at the time of Jesus* (pp. 12–13): context for the conflicts Jesus encountered.
◆ *Extension* (p. 13): *Essenes* – research the Dead Sea Scrolls.
◆ *In the footsteps of Jesus* (p. 14): geographic orientation: selection for the pilgrim journey will show knowledge of the main events of Jesus' life.
◆ **Formative assessment 2**: *Homework* (p. 14): *Copymaster 1: Pilgrim's map.*
◆ **Formative assessment 1**: *Classwork* (p. 14): applying understanding of family and community as a context for faith; aspects of Jewish faith in which Jesus was raised.
◆ **Elsewhere in *Icons***: key people and events in the history of the Jews as the People of God, Y8, 2A; *Other faiths: Judaism*, Passover in Jewish faith today, Y8, 2/3E; Jewish expectations of the Messiah and gospel faith in Jesus the Messiah, Y9, 1C.

Response

Students will evaluate and reflect upon their learning. They will be given opportunities to make connections between their own experience and Revelation. They will:

◆ demonstrate awareness of how an appreciation of background can promote understanding of self and others
◆ show knowledge and understanding of the Jewish context of Jesus' life
◆ show appreciation of how Jesus' social, cultural and religious background is the context for his life and mission.

Response: *Links (p. 15)*

◆ apply learning through reflection: *Pause for thought*
◆ literacy: *Key words*
◆ **Summative assessment**: *Test*
◆ think wider: *Challenge*
◆ opportunity for extended writing/discussion, demonstrate understanding of Jesus' call: *Another step*
◆ recognise relationship of faith and life: *Faith alive*

Resources

Atlas of the Holy Land
Pilgrim guides
Illustrated travel brochures
Bible Alive, Don Henry Wansbrough, John Clare (HarperCollins, 1993) illustrated commentary

For teachers:

Jerusalem CD-ROM (St Paul Multimedia Productions) interactive pilgrimage to the Holy City
The Book of Witness, David Kossoff (Fount, 1971) an older book worth finding for its story telling models

Spiritual and moral links

Understanding our own and others' backgrounds develops respect and appreciation of variety and difference.

Additional activities

◆ A visit to a modern synagogue. This could be a link with the *Other Faiths* section on Judaism this year (p. 70).

◆ Parish link: invite someone who has been on a pilgrimage to the Holy Land to share their experience of walking in the footsteps of Jesus. It would also lay foundations for the work on pilgrimage to come in Y9, 1A.

Doctrinal content

1A: During the greater part of his life Jesus shared the conditions of the vast majority of human beings: a daily life spent without evident greatness, a life of manual labour. His religious life was that of a Jew obedient to the law of God, a life in the community. From this whole period it is revealed to us that Jesus was 'obedient' to his parents and that he 'increased in wisdom and stature, and in favour with God and man'. (*CCC* 531)

Foundations in Year 7

Students should:

◆ show understanding of what it means to belong to a community and be able to identify what gives their school community its distinctive identity

◆ know and understand that the Church finds its identity in Jesus

◆ be able to find their way around the New Testament and know it proclaims the Church's faith in Jesus and his mission.

Links to curriculum directory – KS3

The work in this section relates to the following aspects of the *RECD*. They are revisited and deepened throughout *Icons*. The learning outcomes for this section present the *RECD* for classroom use:

◆ the life and ministry of Jesus, his teaching, parables and miracles; – that the events of the life, death and resurrection of Jesus Christ are at the heart of the Catholic faith; (p. 17 – Jesus Christ, Son of God)

◆ continuity in God's formation of a people from the Old to New Testament; – the Church's understanding of its communion with Jesus. (p. 22 — Church)

For reflection

Question: What cultures shape my daily life?

With Christ, God has injected himself into history. With the birth of Christ, God's reign is now inaugurated in human time. His birth attests that God is now marching with us in history, that we do not go alone.

(Oscar Romero)

To understand Jesus one has to understand the history of the Jewish people and their belief that they were the chosen ones of God who would bring light and salvation to humanity.

(Jean Vanier, *The Gift of Love*)

Catholic teaching

The Son of God … worked with human hands … he thought with a human mind. He acted with a human will, and with a human heart he loved. Born of the Virgin Mary, he has truly been made one of us, like to us in all things except sin. (*Pastoral Constitution on the Church in the world of today*, 22)

The Church also keeps constantly before its eyes the words of the apostle Paul concerning those of his own race: 'and to them belong the adoption as children, the glory, the covenant, the giving of the law, the worship and the promises; to them belong the patriarchs, and of their race, according to the flesh, is Christ, son of the Virgin Mary'. It also recalls that the apostles, the foundations and pillars of the Church were born out of the Jewish people as were many of those first disciples who proclaimed the gospel of Christ to the world. (*Declaration on the Church's relation to non-Christian religions*, 4)

The Son of God could, when he became man, 'increase in wisdom and stature, and in favour with God and man', and would even have to inquire for himself about what one in the human condition can only learn from experience. (*CCC* 472)

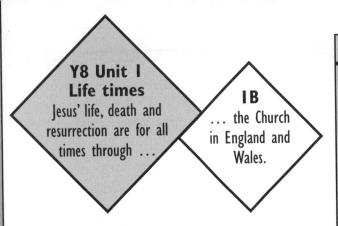

Summary of key learning

The Christian tradition in Britain dates back to the first century AD. **Christianity** came to Britain in **Roman times**. **Celtic missionaries** in the North and West and **missionaries from Rome** in the South preached the Gospel, established **monasteries** and laid the foundations of the Church in Britain. Links with Rome nourished understanding of the **apostolic tradition**. The Church had a significant role at every level in society.

Teaching and learning process: *learning outcomes*

By the end of this section of work, students should:
◆ be able to recognise the importance of its history to every family and nation
◆ know key people and events in the history of the Church in Britain from the first to the fifteenth centuries
◆ have an appreciation of how these have shaped Catholic faith in England and Wales.

At each stage, select activities to fulfil the learning outcomes.

Research

Students will have the opportunity to investigate and reflect upon:
◆ key people, events and times in their family history and why it is important for people to know their roots.

Research

◆ *Family history* (p. 16): links from 1A to the focus here on key people and events; leads on to importance of history for country/nation, as a foundation for study of Church history.
◆ **Diagnostic assessment**: *Check your learning* (p. 16): assesses basic historical learning. (Answers: BC, Before Christ; AD, *Anno Domini*, in the year of the Lord, BCE, Before the common era, CE, common era. Dinosaurs, Romans, Anglo-Saxons, Tudors, Victorians) N.B. *Icons* uses BC and AD for historical numbering.

Revelation

Students will have the opportunity to learn about and reflect upon:
◆ key people, places and events in the history of the Church in Britain from Roman times to pre-Reformation, with a focus on local history
◆ the significance of these for the life of the Church.

Revelation

◆ *The Church in Britain* (pp. 17–19): this overview covers key events and people from the first to the fifteenth centuries. This study encourages understanding of the lived tradition of faith that forms the Church (cf. *CCC* 759). Time spent on the overview prepares students for a choice of individual projects.
N.B. Christianity came to Britain during the Roman occupation. At that time the names England and Wales did not exist. Bishops from Britain were present at Church Councils in Europe. Devotion to St Peter was very popular in Britain and so was the pilgrimage to Rome. There can be an ambiguity about the title 'the Church in Wales' as the Anglican Church describes itself as the Church in Wales.
◆ *Copymasters 2 and 3: Teacher's history notes.*
◆ *Copymaster 4: Source texts from Bede – St Alban, first Christian martyr.*
◆ *Copymaster 5: Source texts from Bede – Caedmon, poet.*
◆ *Village life* (p. 20) opportunities for local projects.
◆ **Formative assessment 2**: *Homework* (p. 20): individual projects.
◆ **Formative assessment 1**: *Classwork* (p. 20): learning from the past.
◆ **Elsewhere in *Icons***: overview of the Reformation and post-Reformation, including some recent Church history, Y9, 1B.

Response

Students will evaluate and reflect upon their learning. They will be given opportunities to make connections between their own experience and Revelation. They will:
◆ demonstrate understanding of the importance of family history
◆ be able to identify key people, places and events in the history of the Church in England and Wales
◆ be able to make some connections between this history and the Church today, and appreciate their significance.

Response: *Links (p. 21)*

◆ think wider and deeper: *Pause for thought*
◆ literacy: *Key words*
◆ **Summative assessment**: *Test*
◆ value of history for the present: *Challenge*
◆ a thirteenth century view: *Faith alive*
◆ opportunity for students' version of Church figures of modern times: *Another step*

Resources

Guide books of some English cathedrals or videos which the local library or teacher centre may be able to obtain

2000 Years: The Christian Faith in Britain (Lion Books, 2000)

Return of the Saints, the Northern saints, narrated by Cardinal Basil Hume (St Paul Multimedia Productions)

For teachers:
The Illustrated Bede, John Marsden (Macmillan, 1989) selections from the text

Spiritual and moral links

Reflecting on what has happened can help us to learn from events.

Additional activities

◆ Contact a local historian or local archaeological society, who can make links to the Christian heritage of the area.

◆ Look at selections from *Return of the Saints*.

◆ Investigate the role of the Church in times of development (e.g. monastic farms) and crisis (e.g. the Black Death).

◆ Cross-curriculum links with the History Department: the influence of communities of monks and nuns, guilds and charters, and the Jews in Britain (1066–1500) are included in KS3 National Curriculum.

Doctrinal content

1B: 'The Father ... determined to call together in a holy Church those who should believe in Christ.' This 'family of God' is gradually formed and takes shape during the stages of human history, in keeping with the Father's plan. (*CCC* 759) The Church is in history, but at the same time she transcends it. It is only 'with the eyes of faith' that one can see her in her visible reality and at the same time in her spiritual reality as bearer of divine life. (*CCC* 770)

Foundations in Year 7

Students should:

◆ appreciate the demands of relationships for building community

◆ know and understand that the first Christians began to build community in response to Jesus' call

◆ know that there are different Christian Churches in England and Wales.

Links to curriculum directory – KS3

The work in this section relates to the following aspects of the *RECD*. They are revisited and deepened throughout *Icons*. The learning outcomes for this section present the *RECD* for classroom use:

◆ the history and development of the Church in Britain; – the main developments in the history of the Church in Britain; (p. 22 – Catholic)

◆ the Church's role as witness in society; – the Church's pastoral role: to be a revelation of God's love and forgiveness, the teacher and servant of the People of God; (p. 22 – Mission)

◆ humanity as created by God; – that Scripture and Tradition reveal God's love, mercy and forgiveness, which meet human faithfulness and sinfulness. (p. 17 – Creation)

For reflection

Question: From what roots do I draw strength?

Only faith can guarantee the blessings that we hope for, or prove the existence of realities that are unseen. It is for their faith that our ancestors are acknowledged.

(Hebrews 11: 1–2)

I can only answer the question 'What am I to do?' if I can answer the prior question 'Of what story or stories do I find myself a part?'

(Alasdair MacIntyre)

Catholic teaching

The Church has to incarnate the gospel in history: Christ by his incarnation committed himself to the particular social and cultural circumstances of the people among whom he lived. This is the original 'inculturation' of the word of God and is the model of all evangelisation by the Church, called to bring the power of the gospel into the very heart of culture and cultures. (*General Directory for Catechesis* 109)

Our words are handed down to us through history, shaped by the tradition which Christians believe is a source of revelation. We do not have to re-create the whole language for God afresh in each little lifetime: it is there and we can enter into it, use it, lean on it, because we know it is true.

(Sara Maitland, *A Big Enough God*)

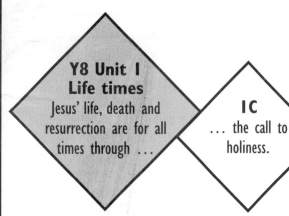

Y8 Unit I Life times
Jesus' life, death and resurrection are for all times through ...

1C
... the call to holiness.

Summary of key learning

Every person has a **vocation**. Each one is **called to share God's life** in a personal way. The **Baptism of Jesus** reveals the **call** of God and the **response** of the **disciple**, the true child of God.

Teaching and learning process: *learning outcomes*

By the end of this section of work, students should:
- understand the importance of a sense of vocation for human life
- know and understand Christian belief that God calls (vocation) and how people respond (search, faith and commitment).

At each stage, select activities to fulfil the learning outcomes.

Research

Students will have the opportunity to investigate and reflect upon:
- the reality of vocation in people's lives: recognising strengths and weaknesses, identifying choices, discerning opportunities, weighing the costs
- how appreciation of vocation contributes to a sense of identity and wholeness.

Revelation

Students will have the opportunity to learn about and reflect upon:
- how Scripture shows people recognising and responding to God's call
- some ways in which Christians today discern God's call for them and the ways they might respond.

Response

Students will evaluate and reflect upon their learning. They will be given opportunities to make connections between their own experience and Revelation. They will:
- be able to evaluate evidence of the importance of vocation in people's lives
- demonstrate some knowledge and understanding of call and response in Scripture
- illustrate their understanding of vocation with examples from today.

Research
- *Work in groups* (p. 22): picture exercise draws out awareness of jobs/careers; introduce key words: *quality, talent, skill, gifted, vocation.*
- *A sense of self* and *Who are you?* (p. 22–23): examines the role of self-awareness in human development and moral formation; key words: *self-esteem, self-knowledge, self-confidence*; provides basis for work to come on conscience in Y8, 2D. 'It is important for every person to be sufficiently present to himself/herself in order to hear and follow the voice of conscience. (*CCC* 1779)
- *Pause for thought* (p. 23): sums up Research: each person is unique and has a unique call from God.

Revelation
- **Diagnostic assessment**: *Check your learning* (p. 23 link to Y7, 3A).
- *Called by God* (pp. 24–25) introduces the concept of discernment of God's call; leads to Scripture-based study of Jesus' responses. *One*: age of twelve – 'coming of age', Bar Mitzvah, entitled to read from the Law; searching for God's way; learns the Temple is not the place now, and returns to live ordinary life for about 18 years. *Two*: N.B. links to the Trinity in imagery – Mark proclaims Jesus, sent by the Father (voice) and working in the power of the Spirit (dove). *Three*: temptations evoke the Old Testament imagery of God's salvation (e.g. bread – life, spiritual nature of humanity) reveal the kind of Messiah Jesus was to be and the new Israel (the Church) living by the word of God, trusting God's promises, worshipping and serving God alone.
- **Formative assessment 1**: *Classwork* (p. 25).
- *Mother of Jesus* (p. 25): reinforces understanding of personal vocation and appreciation of Mary as model of Christian life. (cf. *CCC* 967–968)
- *Called to be ... What? How?* (p. 26): reinforces understanding of the importance of discernment through what life brings and gives.
- *Worldwide mission* (p. 26): introduces global dimension; opportunity to research the missionary vocation of all Christians.
- **Formative assessment 2**: *Homework* (p. 26): understanding of vocation.
- **Elsewhere in *Icons***: Human, spiritual and moral development continues in Y8, 1D, 2B, 2D, 3A and in Y9, 1B, 2A, 2/3E; marriage and priesthood in Y9, 3C.

Response: *Links (p. 27)*
- think wider and deeper: *Pause for thought*
- literacy: *Key words*
- **Summative assessment**: *Test*
- individual/Christian vocation: *Pause for thought*
- self-development: *Challenge*
- opportunity for extended discussion/writing: *Another step*
- recognising faith in practice: *Faith alive*

Tips for teachers

Resources

Anne Frank: the Diary of a Young Girl (Puffin, 1997) diary of a teenager who discovered her talent for living while in hiding during the Second World War

'Will You Come and Follow Me?', *A Touching Place*, John Bell and Graham Maule (Wild Goose Publications, 1986)

For teachers:
Follow Your Dream, Peter Hannan SJ (Columba Press, 1998)

Spiritual and moral links

Each one of us needs others to help us to understand what we are called to be.

Additional activities

◆ Create a personal time capsule. Include a record of the talents for living you have now and how you hope to use them. At this time say what, if any, sense you have of your vocation. You might include a statement from a friend about the talents they see in you and how they hope you will use them. Choose a secure place to store your capsule and plan to open it ten years on.

◆ Cross-curricular link: with the help of the Art Department find some paintings of the Baptism of Jesus. Which do you prefer and why? Or, create your own gallery of Baptism of Jesus paintings.

◆ Read *Anne Frank: the Diary of a Young Girl*.

◆ Start or revive a diary/journal of your own.

Doctrinal content

1C: The vocation of humanity is to show forth the image of God and to be transformed into the image of the Father's only Son. This vocation takes a personal form since each of us is called to enter into the divine beatitude; it also concerns the human community as a whole. (*CCC* 1877)

Foundations in Year 7

Students should:

◆ understand how self-esteem, self-knowledge and respect contribute to the growth and development of each person

◆ be able to identify and describe some ways in which people give their lives for others

◆ know and understand Christian belief that the gift of life is the beginning of a loving relationship – covenant – with God and that human beings have a unique place in creation

◆ appreciate that the creative energy and imagination of human beings is evidence of their spiritual nature

◆ know and understand Jesus' call to discipleship

◆ know how Mary responded to God and appreciate why the Church honours her.

Links to curriculum directory – KS3

The work in this section relates to the following aspects of the *RECD*. They are revisited and deepened throughout *Icons*. The learning outcomes for this section present the *RECD* for classroom use:

◆ the Old Testament understanding of life as a gift which requires a response; – the gift of life is God's covenant with each person; – of commitment and response; (p. 38 – law, grace, sin)

◆ continuity in God's formation of a People from the Old to New Testament; – the Church's understanding of, and teaching about, the roles of Father, Son and Holy Spirit in the life and mission of the Church; (p. 22 – Church)

◆ the Church's understanding of vocation: exemplified in Mary, lived by local and national saints and communities; – the Church's understanding and teaching about vocation and the need for a personal response to God; – the example, role and privileges of Mary. (p. 22 – one and holy)

For reflection

Question: By what do I measure my response to life?

There are two words used a great deal by Jesus in the gospels. One is 'come' and the other is 'go'. It's no use coming unless you go, and it's no use going unless you come.

(Anon.)

I like the concept of man being in search of God. Slowly we come to realise that it is only one way of speaking of our response to God's search for us. That is where the initiative lies. God in search of man reveals Himself in a way which the created world cannot. It is a special kind of revelation. It reached its high point when the Son of God became man.

(Basil Hume, *To Be a Pilgrim*)

Catholic teaching

All the faithful, whatever their condition or rank, are called to the fullness of the Christian life and the perfection of charity. And this sanctity is conducive to a more human way of living even in society here on earth. (*Dogmatic Constitution on the Church*, 40)

Everyone is called to enter the kingdom. First announced to the children of Israel, this messianic kingdom is intended to accept people of all nations. To enter it, one must first accept Jesus' word. (*CCC* 543)

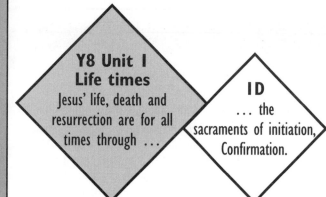

**Y8 Unit I
Life times**
Jesus' life, death and resurrection are for all times through ...

ID
... the sacraments of initiation, Confirmation.

> ### Summary of key learning
> **Confirmation** is one of the **sacraments of initiation**. The **laying on of hands** and **anointing** with the oil of **chrism** confer the **gift of the Holy Spirit** who empowers people to live as disciples.

Teaching and learning process: *learning outcomes*

By the end of this section of work, students should:
- appreciate how many gifts contribute to the life of a community
- know and understand how the sacrament of Confirmation deepens Christian initiation and vocation
- know and understand the significance of anointing as a symbolic act that acknowledges and consecrates vocation.

Research
Students will have the opportunity to investigate and reflect upon:
- how people value and share the gifts that benefit communities
- ways in which communities and society recognise and honour people's gifts.

Revelation
Students will have the opportunity to learn about and reflect upon:
- the rites of the sacrament of Confirmation and its place in the Christian journey
- the significance of anointing in the sacraments of Baptism and Confirmation
- passages from Scripture that show the importance of anointing as a symbol of dedication to God.

Response
Students will evaluate and reflect upon their learning. They will be given opportunities to make connections between their own experience and Revelation. They will:
- illustrate some of the ways in which people value and share gifts that benefit communities
- be able to describe the rite of the Sacrament of Confirmation and its significance
- demonstrate knowledge and understanding of anointing as a symbol of dedication.

At each stage, select activities to fulfil the learning outcomes.

Research
- *The Jones family* (p. 28): focuses on effort and co-operation.
- *Think and talk* (p. 28): follow on work on the value and use of unique gifts and talents. Links to be made: between gifts and service, and to 1C – vocation.

Revelation
- *A call to live by the Spirit* (p. 29): in Y7, 1D, students learned about the three sacraments of initiation. This section focuses on the rites of Confirmation.
- **Diagnostic assessment**: *Check your learning* (p. 29).
- Focus on the principal actions and symbols of the rite and what these reveal of God's action and the human response. Links to Scripture: Jesus' promise (John 14: 16–17, 26) and to Y7, 3B. The coming of the Holy Spirit transformed the apostles and confirmed them in their mission.
  N.B., 'a sacramental celebration is woven from signs and symbols' (*CCC* 1145); 'a sacramental celebration is a meeting of God's children with their Father in Christ and the Holy Spirit which takes the form of a dialogue through actions and words' (*CCC* 1153).
- *Copymaster 6: Prayers of Confirmation*.
- **Formative assessment 1**: *Classwork* (p. 29).
- *Do you remember?* and *Group talk* (p. 30): links back to Baptism and develops awareness of the variety of practice in the celebration of Confirmation.
- Symbols (pp. 30–31): oil of chrism and Christian name; make links between *chrism, Christ, Christ crucified* and *Christian*.
- The gifts of the Spirit (p. 31): links back to Y7, 3B (p. 83).
- **Formative assessment 2**: *Homework* (p. 31).
- *Extension* (p. 32): builds on Y7 work on baptismal anointing with chrism and using the Spirit's gifts in sharing Christ's mission as priest, prophet and king.
- **Elsewhere in *Icons***: the Christian journey, Y9, 1A; the power of the Holy Spirit Y9, 3B; the Church's sacraments of service, Y9, 3C.

Response: *Links (p. 33)*
- apply learning: *Letter to parish priest*
- literacy: *Key words*
- **Summative assessment**: *Test*
- reflect deeper: *Pause for thought* and *Challenge*
- opportunity for extended discussion/writing: *Another step*
- reflect and empathise: *Faith alive*

Tips for teachers

Resources

The Sacraments of Christian Initiation Series, Turvey Abbey (St Paul Multimedia Productions) posters and booklet
It is useful to know what programmes are used by local parishes for sacramental preparation.

For teachers:
Sacraments Revisited, What do they mean today?, Liam Kelly (DLT, 1998)

Spiritual and moral links

The importance of celebrating key moments that mark periods of growth and development.

Additional activities

◆ Use the title, *The best age for Confirmation is …*, for a class debate or extended essay writing.

◆ Interview someone who has been, or is soon to be, confirmed. Plan your questions. Pool answers and produce a survey report for a school newsletter or magazine.

◆ Design banners to decorate a church on Confirmation day.

Doctrinal content

1D: Confirmation perfects Baptismal grace; it is the sacrament which gives the Holy Spirit, in order to root us more deeply in the divine filiation, incorporate us more firmly into Christ, strengthen our bond with the Church, associate us more closely with her mission, and help us bear witness to the Christian faith in words accompanied by deeds. (*CCC* 1316)

Foundations in Year 7

Students should:

◆ appreciate how people are welcomed and initiated into communities

◆ know and understand that the Church is a community of believers

◆ know what a sacrament is and that the Catholic Church celebrates Christian initiation in three sacraments: Baptism, Confirmation and Eucharist

◆ know how Christians recognise and name the creative power of the Holy Spirit in the world.

Links to curriculum directory – KS3

The work in this section relates to the following aspects of the *RECD*. They are revisited and deepened throughout *Icons*. The learning outcomes for this section present the *RECD* for classroom use:

◆ the seven sacraments of the Church; the universal value of some signs and symbols; – the essential elements of the rites, the symbols used and their significance; – the place of universal signs and symbols in the life of the Church; (p. 30 – sacraments)

◆ the significance of the rites of Confirmation and the Church's teaching about the gifts of the Holy Spirit; – Confirmation deepens a personal response to the call and grace of Baptism; (p. 30 – Baptism, Confirmation and the Eucharist)

◆ the Old Testament understanding of life as a gift which requires a response; – that the gift of life is God's covenant with each person; (p. 38 – law, grace, sin)

◆ the role of the Holy Spirit in the Old and New Testament; – that the Holy Spirit guides and leads the People of God into the truth of the gospel. (p. 17 – the Holy Spirit)

For reflection

Question: What keeps me going from day to day?

Likeness to God comes only from the Spirit.
(St Irenaeus)

To obtain the gift of Christian holiness is the work of a lifetime.
(John Henry Newman)

To penetrate the secrets of nature requires powerful, precise instruments. To penetrate the secrets of the presence of God hidden within ourselves and history, we need a power beyond our own. To search out the realm of the invisible we need a light the rays of which are more delicate, more piercing than infrared. This power, this light, is the Holy Spirit who alone 'explores the depths of God'.
(Cardinal Suenens, *A New Pentecost*, DLT, 1975)

Catholic teaching

The word 'Christ' comes from the Greek translation of the Hebrew 'Messiah' which means 'anointed'. It became the name proper to Jesus only because he accomplished perfectly the divine mission that 'Christ' signifies. The Messiah had to be anointed by the Spirit as king, priest and prophet. (*CCC* 436–438) The name Christian implies discipleship and commitment to Christ and the gospel.

From the time of the apostles, becoming a Christian has been accomplished by a journey and initiation in several stages. This journey can be covered rapidly or slowly, but certain essential elements will always have to be present: proclamation of the Word, acceptance of the Gospel entailing conversion, profession of faith, Baptism itself, the outpouring of the Holy Spirit, and admission to Eucharistic communion. (*CCC* 1229)

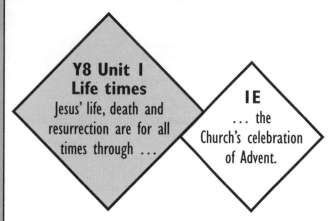

Y8 Unit I
Life times
Jesus' life, death and resurrection are for all times through ...

IE
... the Church's celebration of Advent.

Summary of key learning

Advent remembers and celebrates the way God formed the Chosen People through the **prophets**. They called people to trust in God's promises and to be faithful to God's law. **John the Baptist** is a key figure in the Advent Liturgy. He prepared people for the coming of Jesus. The Church is called to be ready to welcome Christ the Lord.

Teaching and learning process: *learning outcomes*

By the end of this section of work, students should:
- appreciate the significance of elements of time – past, present and future – in people's lives
- know more about the Church's season of Advent as a time of remembering, waiting, preparation and anticipation
- know about and understand the role of prophets in Scripture.

At each stage, select activities to fulfil the learning outcomes.

Research

Students will have the opportunity to investigate and reflect upon:
- *the importance of memory, celebration and expectation.*

Research
- Focus in this section is on Advent. Christmas will be part of the whole school celebrations and links may be made to Y7 work on Christmas.
- *Many happy returns* (p. 34): birthdays are times when past, present and future come together.
- *Copymaster 7: Birthday scene*: drama as optional starting point.
- **Diagnostic assessment**: *Check your learning* (p. 34): assesses prior learning about Church's cycle of feasts and seasons. Link to Y7, 1E.

Revelation

Students will have the opportunity to learn about and reflect upon:
- *what Advent celebrates about Jesus: past, present and future*
- *the role of the prophets in Scripture: Old Testament, John the Baptist*
- *expectancy and mystery of this Church season.*

Revelation
- *Advent* (p. 35): focus on the meaning of Advent leads to Church's Advent figure, John the Baptist. Group work builds a profile of John using gospel references for the lectionary Advent cycles.
- *Be ready!* (p. 36): explores John's message and makes links to the present.
- **Formative assessment 2**: *Homework* (p. 36).
- *Someone is coming* (p. 36): focuses on the Church's use of Old Testament prophecies: 'through the prophets, God forms his people in the hope of salvation, in the expectation of a new and everlasting covenant intended for all, to be written on their hearts' (*CCC* 64). Leads to opportunity for creative presentation of Advent message in:
- **Formative assessment 1**: *Classwork* (p. 36).
- *Be alert!* (p. 37): focuses on Advent mood of expectancy and God who surprises. The hymn 'God beyond all dreams', offers the chance to explore the mystery of God through imagery; and to build on Y7, 1E – The Word made flesh. The mystery of God in creation (*CCC* 339, 341) in human persons (*CCC* 363, 365) by the power of the Spirit in Jesus (*CCC* 244, 2466) and in the Church (*CCC* 775, 776).
- **Elsewhere in *Icons***: the relationship of Advent and Christmas, Y9, 1E.

Response

Students will evaluate and reflect upon their learning. They will be given opportunities to make connections between their own experience and Revelation. They will:
- *be able to explain and illustrate the role of memory and expectation for the future in celebration*
- *be able to explain the importance of Advent in the Church's year and the spirit of this season.*

Response: *Links (p. 38)*
- explore Church tradition: *Pause for thought*
- literacy: *Key words*
- question and think deeper: *Challenge*
- **Summative assessment**: *Test*
- empathise and interpret Church's season: *Faith alive*

Resources

Liturgical Calendar
An Advent wreath
Joyful Hope (St Paul Multimedia Productions)
liturgical posters designed at Turvey Abbey, slides
and booklet also available

For teachers:
Coming Christ in Advent, Raymond Brown (The
Liturgical Press, 1988)

Spiritual and moral links

Reflecting on the past, making the most of the
present and hoping in the future are all part of
human experience.

Additional activities

◆ Drama: create an Advent dialogue in words and
music, featuring people you have learned about
in this section of work.

◆ Involve Year 8 students in planning and leading
the school Advent service/celebrations this
year.

◆ Write an Advent reflection/prayer in three
parts beginning: *Once… Now…When…*

◆ 'Christ comes to take away the darkness.'
Explore images of waiting/expectancy,
light/darkness, good/evil in seasonal
traditions, carols, stories (e.g. Scrooge) and
pantomimes.

Doctrinal content

1E: The coming of God's Son to earth is an event of such immensity that God willed to prepare for it over
centuries. He makes everything converge on Christ: all the rituals and sacrifices, figures and symbols of the 'First
Covenant'. He announces him through the mouths of the prophets who succeeded one another in Israel.
Moreover, he awakens in the hearts of the pagans a dim expectation of this coming. (*CCC* 552)

Foundations in Year 7

Students should:

◆ show understanding and appreciation
of ways in which times and seasons
give shape to human life

◆ have reflected upon the symbolism of
darkness and light

◆ have learned that the times and
seasons of the Christian year
remember and celebrate the life,
death and resurrection of Jesus

◆ show understanding of what the
season of Christmas celebrates and
Mary's role in the Christmas event.

Links to curriculum directory – KS3

The work in this section relates to the following aspects of the *RECD*.
They are revisited and deepened throughout *Icons*. The learning
outcomes for this section present the *RECD* for classroom use:

◆ the concept of the Messiah in the Old and New Testament; –
Jesus is God become man so that human beings might share the
life of God; (p. 17 – Jesus Christ)

◆ the role of the prophets – their call to faithfulness, repentance,
justice and compassion for all especially the poor and weak; –
the Church's mission to proclaim Good News to all ages and all
people; (p. 17 – the Holy Spirit)

◆ the mission of Jesus as revealed in the New Testament with
particular reference to his priestly, prophetic and kingly roles; –
that as priest, prophet and king Jesus proclaims the kingdom of
God. (p. 22 – apostolic)

For reflection

Question: What
do I mean by
justice? How do
I do justice?

Justice is the firm disposition to give
others their due. It is the virtue by which
we *adjust*. We try to reach a morally
acceptable way of living in common,
making way for love and friendship.
(Robert Ombres OP)

Prophets are poets speaking the
word a new way to let there be
light.
(Source unknown)

The future is the
most expensive
luxury in the world.
(Thornton Wilder,
The Matchmaker)

We only know
who God is and
who we are
when we hope.
(Karl Rahner)

In truth I tell you, of all the children
born to women, there has never been
anyone greater than John the Baptist.
(Matthew 11: 11)

Catholic teaching

The patriarchs, prophets and certain other
Old Testament figures have been and
always will be honoured as saints in all the
Church's liturgical traditions.

Through the prophets, God forms his
people in the hope of salvation, in the
expectation of a new and everlasting
Covenant intended for all to be written on
their hearts. The prophets proclaim a
radical redemption of the People of God,
purification from all their infidelities, a
salvation which will include all the nations.
Above all, the poor and humble of the Lord
will bear this hope. Such holy women as
Sarah, Rebecca, Rachel, Miriam, Deborah,
Hannah, Judith and Esther kept alive the
hope of Israel's salvation. The purest figure
among them is Mary. (*CCC* 61, 64)

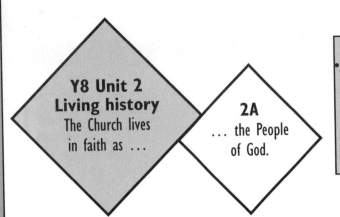

Y8 Unit 2 Living history
The Church lives in faith as ...

2A ... the People of God.

Summary of key learning
Over many generations God formed the **Chosen People**. The **Exodus** from Egypt and the **covenant** at Sinai are key events in their history, preparing for the **new and everlasting covenant**. The retelling of this story is an important part of the Church's Easter Vigil.

Teaching and learning process: *learning outcomes*

By the end of this section of work, students should:
- appreciate the significance of a name
- know and understand the significance of the Exodus for the Church
- know more about and appreciate what it means to call the Church 'the People of God'.

At each stage, select activities to fulfil the learning outcomes.

Research

Students will have the opportunity to investigate and reflect upon:
- how groups and organisations get their names and the significance of names.

Research
- *What's in a name?* (p. 39): brand names as a way to explore the importance of names; explore the power of a name to sum up a group and establish a sense of identity.
- *The people of ...* (p. 39): introduces the concept of 'people' as a collective identity.
- **Diagnostic assessment**: *Check your learning* (p. 39): assesses familiarity with some names and images used of the Church.

Revelation

Students will have the opportunity to learn about and reflect upon:
- the Exodus experience as a key event for the church: in the Easter Liturgy
- what it means to call the Church 'People of God': covenant.

Revelation
- *The People of God* (pp. 40–41): timeline as overview of the salvation history of God's People in the Old Testament; focus on the covenant God makes with Abraham and his descendants; and key figures and events in the life of the chosen people. The Exodus and covenant of Sinai make Israel 'the priestly people of God, called by the name of the Lord and the first to hear the word of God, the people of 'elder brethren' in the faith of Abraham'; the people God forms in expectation of a new and everlasting Covenant. (*CCC* 62–64)
- *Escape to freedom* (pp. 42–43): *Group task one: The Exodus*: provides a foundation for understanding the symbolism and narrative of the Easter vigil. *Group task two: a new Covenant*: focuses on the retelling of salvation history during the Easter Vigil – exploration should highlight God's faithfulness and human search and journey. Scope for links to the liturgy and creative work using drama, posters, mime, music is offered in *Formative assessments 1 and 2*.
- **Formative assessment 1**: *Classwork* (p. 43).
- **Formative assessment 2**: *Homework* (p. 43): *Copymaster 8*. Focus on the Church as the New People of God.
- **Elsewhere in *Icons***: the Church as the communion of saints, Y8, 3D; called to care for the common good, Y9, 3A; the Kingdom of God Jesus proclaimed, Y8, 3C; a present and future reality, Y9, 3D.

Response

Students will evaluate and reflect upon their learning. They will be given opportunities to make connections between their own experience and Revelation. They will:
- demonstrate appreciation of the significance and power of names
- demonstrate knowledge and understanding of the Exodus as a key event for the church
- be able to explain 'People of God' as a name for the Church
- demonstrate knowledge and understanding of the significance of the covenant for the People of God.

Response: *Links (p. 44)*
- reflect on richness of imagery: *Pause for thought*
- literacy: *Key words*
- question and think deeper: *Challenge*
- relate doctrine and experience: *Faith alive* and *Pause for thought*
- **Summative assessment**: *Test*
- opportunity for extended discussion/writing: *Another step*

Tips for teachers

Resources

Godspell, the musical, CD or video – focus on the surprise of Jesus and his message and the unexpected fulfilment

Testament, the Bible in Animation (St Paul Multimedia Productions) video – sections about Abraham and Moses

For teachers:

A pilgrim God for a pilgrim people, Denis Carrol (Gill and Macmillan, 1988)

Spiritual and moral links

Privilege and responsibility are part of the human condition.

Additional activities

◆ Cross-curricular links:
   Music: Create musical themes for key moments or people in the story of the Old Testament People of God. Use your themes with words to tell the story at a year assembly.

◆ Design Technology: Create 2D or 3D images for the Exodus Experience. Or, write a game plan for a video game called *Exodus*.

Doctrinal content

2A: The word 'Church' (Latin *ecclesia*, from the Greek *ek-kalein*, to 'call out of') means a convocation or an assembly. It designates the assemblies of people, usually for a religious purpose. *Ekkelsia* is used frequently in the Greek Old Testament for the assembly of the Chosen People before God, above all for their assembly on Mount Sinai where Israel received the Law and was established by God as his holy people. By calling itself 'Church', the first community of Christian believers recognised itself as heir to that assembly. In the Church, God is 'calling together' his people from all the ends of the earth. (*CCC* 751)

Foundations in Year 7

Students should:

◆ show understanding of what it means to belong to a community and be able to identify what gives their school community its distinctive identity

◆ know and understand that the Church is a community of believers, local and worldwide

◆ know and understand the Church's role as witness to the resurrection

◆ know and appreciate the Easter call to Christians to live a new life.

Links to curriculum directory – KS3

The work in this section relates to the following aspects of the *RECD*. They are revisited and deepened throughout *Icons*. The learning outcomes for this section present the *RECD* for classroom use:

◆ passages from Scripture which speak of God ... – how Scripture names God; (p. 17 – trinity)

◆ the life and ministry of Jesus, his teaching, parables and miracles; – that Jesus is God become man so that human beings might share the life of God; (p. 17 – Jesus Christ, Son of God)

◆ the Church's role as witness in society ... – that in the church Christ's mission continues. (p. 22 – mission)

For reflection

Question: How does my life name the Church?

The image of the People of God lays stress on the human characteristics of the church. We, the People of God, are Church because we respond to God's call, his invitation. And we respond with what we are and with what we have. We bring our humanity to this task, with its creativity and ingenuity, its strengths and weaknesses, its goodness and its waywardness. We are not perfect as we come to him who alone is able to make us fruitful.

(Basil Hume, *Towards a Civilisation of Love*)

All of us together make up God's people. All our varied gifts and responsibilities must conspire harmoniously in the one Spirit who animates the whole Church.

(John Paul II, *Message to the National Pastoral Congress*, Liverpool, 1980)

Catholic teaching

At all times and in every nation whoever fears God and does what is right is acceptable to God. It has pleased God, however, to sanctify and save men and women not individually and without regard for what binds them together, but to set them up as a people who would acknowledge him in truth and serve him in holiness. Therefore he chose the people of Israel as a people for himself, and he made a covenant with them and instructed them step by step, making himself and his intention known to them in their history and sanctifying them for himself. All this took place as a preparation and a figure of that new and perfect covenant which was to be struck with Christ, and of the more complete revelation that was to be made through the Word of God himself made flesh.

(*Dogmatic Constitution on the Church* 9)

(See also *CCC* 781–786.)

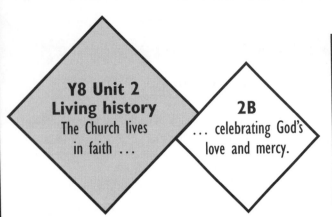

Y8 Unit 2
Living history
The Church lives
in faith …

2B
… celebrating God's
love and mercy.

Summary of key learning

Through the **sacraments of healing**: the **Anointing of the Sick** and **Reconciliation**, the Church continues the mission of Jesus to bring **God's mercy, forgiveness and healing** to all, especially those who are lost and marginalised. Lent is the special season when Christians are called to turn away from sin and prepare to celebrate God's mercy and forgiveness at Easter.

Teaching and learning process: *learning outcomes*

By the end of this section of work, students should:
- appreciate the reality of human imperfection and sinfulness and its consequences within the Church
- know and understand how the Church receives God's love, mercy, forgiveness and healing in two sacraments: Anointing of the Sick and Reconciliation.

At each stage, select activities to fulfil the learning outcomes.

Research

Students will have the opportunity to investigate and reflect upon:
- situations which show that people are in search of wholeness
- the consequences of the breakdown of relationships.

Revelation

Students will have the opportunity to learn about and reflect upon:
- the spiritual struggle to be faithful to the Gospel
- God's gifts of love, mercy, and forgiveness in the sacraments of healing: Anointing of the Sick and Reconciliation.

Response

Students will evaluate and reflect upon their learning. They will be given opportunities to make connections between their own experience and Revelation. They will:
- be able to identify some causes and consequences of evil and sin in the world
- know and understand that the human struggle is spiritual and physical
- demonstrate knowledge and understanding of the Church's sacraments of healing.

Research

- *When it all goes wrong* (p. 45): requires sensitive use; emphasise the reality of the human struggle to live in relationships, true to human and personal vocation; link to Y8, 1C.
- *What's behind the headlines?* (p. 45): widens range of examples; leads into Revelation, the concept of personal sin and the challenge to choose God's way.

Revelation

- *'Yes' to new life* (p. 46): link to work on covenant and exodus that showed God's faithful love and mercy. The Catechism stresses that to try to understand what sin is we must first recognise the profound relation of humanity to God. (*CCC* 386)
- **Diagnostic assessment**: *Check your learning* (p. 46): assesses recall of learning in Year 8, 2A and Year 7, 1D and understanding of new life in Christ.
- *Lent: a spotlight on faithfulness* and *Turn away from Sin! Turn away from what?* (pp. 46–47): focus on spiritual struggle, the need for self-discipline, repentance and penance, and how these support gospel living.
- *Sacraments of healing* (pp. 48–49): develops the concept of sin as denial of community – sickness as isolation from community and healing the renewal of and restoration to relationship with God in the communion of the Church; focus on words and actions of the sacraments (cf. *CCC* 1145, 1153). *Reconciliation* – recall Y7, 2D. *Anointing of the Sick* – focus on celebration of the sacrament during Mass. Using Scripture passages (p. 49), focus on 'restored to'.
  Copymasters 9 and 11: Prayers from the Rite of Reconciliation and *Anointing of the Sick within Mass.*
- *Think and talk* (p. 48): leads to **Formative assessment 2**: *Homework* (p. 48): *Copymaster 10: Recognising evil.*
- *Class project: HCPT – The Pilgrimage Trust* (p. 50). Focus on God's love in prayer and sacraments and on loving service.
- **Formative assessment 1**: *Classwork* (p. 50): Fill in the blanks exercise; answers:
  The gifts of the Sacraments of **Reconciliation** *and the Anointing of the* **Sick** *are God's* **love** *and mercy in times of struggle.* **Lent** *is a time to recognise the damage* **sin** *does to relationship with* **God** *and with* **others**. *The laying on of* **hands** *and anointing with* **oil** *are* **signs** *of God's love,* **comfort** *and* **strength**.
- **Elsewhere in Icons**: the Church's interpretation of the Genesis account of the origin of sin (original sin) and Church teaching about examination of conscience, Y8, 2D; gospel values, Y9, 2B, 2C, 2/3E and Unit 3.

Response: *Links (p. 51)*

- literacy: *Key words*
- **Summative assessment**: *Test*
- reflect and apply learning: *Pause for thought*
- question and think deeper: *Challenge*
- opportunity for extended discussion/writing: *Another step*
- relate learning to belief: *Faith alive*

Resources

Sacraments of Healing and Growth (St Paul Multimedia Productions)
four liturgical posters – Reconciliation, Sacrament of the Sick,
Marriage, Holy Orders – and 24-page booklet
A Lourdes Video from HCPT – The Pilgrimage Trust (Contact: 100A
High Street, Banstead, Surrey SM7 2RB)

For teachers:
Sacraments Revisited, What do they mean today?, Liam Kelly (DLT, 1998)

Spiritual and moral links

Every human being needs support and hope in times of struggle.

Additional activities

◆ Invite the school chaplain or a
   priest to share a question and
   answer session on the
   Sacraments of Healing.

◆ Design symbols for a clip art
   CD-ROM for the Sacraments
   of Healing. Include brief
   notes to help someone
   understand about these
   sacraments.

Doctrinal content

2B: The Lord Jesus Christ, physician of our souls and bodies, who forgave the sins of the paralytic and restored
him to bodily health, has willed that his Church continue, in the power of the Holy Spirit, his work of healing and
salvation, even among her own members. This is the purpose of the two Sacraments of Healing, the Sacrament
of Penance and the Sacrament of Anointing of the Sick (*CCC* 1421).

Foundations in Year 7

Students should:

◆ understand and appreciate the
   vital part forgiveness and
   reconciliation can play in change

◆ know and understand the
   Church's Sacrament of
   Reconciliation as a call to, and
   celebration of, change

◆ understand that the New
   Testament proclaims Jesus the
   Saviour.

Links to curriculum directory – KS3

The work in this section relates to the following aspects of the *RECD*.
They are revisited and deepened throughout *Icons*. The learning
outcomes for this section present the *RECD* for classroom use:

◆ sources of conflict in self and society and the need for healing and
   peace; – the human need for reconciliation and healing; – the place
   and significance of penance and forgiveness in Christian life; (p. 30
   reconciliation and the anointing of the sick)

◆ the gospel accounts of Jesus' compassion in his words and his
   healing miracles; the pattern of forgiveness in the prayer Jesus gave
   his Church; – Jesus came for the healing of all people; (*ibid.*)

◆ the rites of the Sacrament of the Anointing of the Sick and their
   significance; – Christian responsibility to care for the sick and those
   in need. (*ibid.*)

For reflection

Question: When I
recognise a need
for healing where
do I look first?

I don't think we should
consider the problem
[of good and evil] at all
until we realise that
we are sinners.

(Vincent McNabb)

While in other sciences the instruments you
use are things external to yourself (things like
microscopes and telescopes), the instrument
through which you see God is your whole self.
And if a man's self is not kept clean and bright,
his glimpse of God will be blurred – like the
moon seen through a dirty telescope.

(C. S. Lewis)

So he left the place and went back to his father.
While he was still a long way off, his father saw
him and was moved with pity. He ran to the boy,
clasped him in his arms and kissed him.

(Luke 15: 20)

Catholic teaching

Through the sacraments of Christian initiation, we
receive the new life of Christ. Now we carry this
life 'in earthen vessels', and it remains 'hidden with
Christ in God'. We are still in our 'earthly tent',
subject to suffering, illness and death. This new life
as a child of God can be weakened and even lost
by sin. The Lord Jesus Christ, physician of our
souls and bodies, who forgave the sins of the
paralytic and restored him to bodily health, has
willed that his church continue, in the power of the
Holy Spirit, his work of healing and salvation, even
among her own members. This is the purpose of
the two sacraments of healing. (*CCC* 1420–1)

[This sacrament is] called the Sacrament of
Reconciliation, because it imparts to the sinner the
love of God who reconciles: 'Be reconciled to
God.' He who lives by God's merciful love is ready
to respond to the Lord's call: 'Go, first be
reconciled to your brother'. (*CCC* 1424)

The Church believes and confesses that among the
seven sacraments there is one especially intended
to strengthen those who are being tried by illness.
(*CCC* 1511)

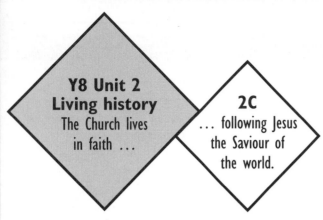

**Y8 Unit 2
Living history**
The Church lives
in faith ...

2C
... following Jesus
the Saviour of
the world.

> ### Summary of key learning
> Luke's gospel focuses on Jesus the **Saviour of all people**. His life, death and resurrection are actions that **save** the world **from sin and death** and **for life that is eternal**. The Church continues Christ's mission.

Teaching and learning process: *learning outcomes*

By the end of this section of work, students should:
◆ appreciate the need for salvation in the world
◆ know and understand how Luke's gospel presents Jesus, the Universal Saviour
◆ have an appreciation of the Christian challenge to be 'one world'.

At each stage, select activities to fulfil the learning outcomes.

Research

Students will have the opportunity to investigate and reflect upon:
◆ how people, places and situations may need 'to be saved' in different ways
◆ what this has to say about the ways in which people understand 'being saved' and 'salvation'.

Research
◆ *It's the way we speak* and *It's the way things happen* (p. 52): explore the concept of 'being saved'; students should understand that the way to safety often requires going through the danger or pain.
◆ **Diagnostic assessment**: *Check your learning* (p. 52): assesses recall of learning in Year 7, 1B and general level of grasp of Christian understanding of 'salvation'.

Revelation

Students will have the opportunity to learn about and reflect upon:
◆ how Luke, through his gospel, presents Jesus as Saviour for all
◆ how belief in Jesus the Saviour has inspired the Church's mission to all peoples
◆ people and organisations that work to promote understanding that we are 'one world'.

Revelation
◆ *The Christian way* (p. 53): develops Christian understanding of 'salvation'. Links to be made to Mark's understanding of Jesus' mission in the gospel account of his baptism, Y8, 1C; also to Exodus and the new Covenant, Y8, 2A.
◆ *Luke* (pp. 53–54): introduces Luke's gospel and its focus on Jesus as Saviour for all peoples. Aspects of salvation to explore in the passages from Luke: the woman with the haemorrhage – saved from excommunication; the widow – saved from mourning; the boy – saved from personal disintegration; the woman taken in adultery – saved from sin; Levi – saved from being an oppressor.
◆ *Saved for ever* (p. 54): deepens understanding of salvation *from* sin and *for* life that is with God for ever.
◆ **Formative assessment 1**: *Classwork* (p. 54).
◆ *One world* (p. 55): focus on Luke's second book, *Acts*, as the story of how the good news was carried to all nations, and leads to the good news in the present day.
◆ *Class project: One World Week* (p. 55): research work.
◆ **Formative assessment 2**: *Homework* (p. 55).
◆ **Elsewhere in *Icons***: the challenge of Christian unity, Y8, 2/3E; the kingdom that is for all, Y8, 3C; Jesus' imagery in the gospel; the kingdom now and forever, Y9, 3D.

Response

Students will evaluate and reflect upon their learning. They will be given opportunities to make connections between their own experience and Revelation. They will:
◆ be able to identify and explain some different levels of salvation
◆ demonstrate knowledge, understanding and appreciation of Luke's presentation of Jesus as Saviour for all
◆ reflect on some ways in which belief in Jesus the Saviour of the World challenges Christians today
◆ be able to identify and illustrate some work for 'one world'.

Response: *Links (p. 56)*
◆ reflect and apply learning: *Pause for thought*
◆ literacy: *Key words*
◆ **Summative assessment**: *Test*
◆ question and think deeper: *Challenge*
◆ relate to liturgy and prayer: *Faith alive*
◆ opportunity for extended discussion/writing: *Another step*

Resources

In the Footsteps of Christ (St Paul Multimedia Productions) videos nos. 5 and 6

For teachers:

'Jesus, Saviour and Son of God', Monika Hellwig in *Contemporary Catholic Theology: a Reader*, ed. Hayes and Gearon (Gracewing, 1998)

Spiritual and moral links

The challenge of living in a society that does not acknowledge its need of salvation.

Additional activities

◆ Scrooge in *A Christmas Carol* by Charles Dickens, offers another approach to the concept of 'being saved'. Use extracts from a video of *A Christmas Carol* to explore his story.

◆ Have a collection of 'Jesus Saves' stickers. Available in Christian bookshops. Use as basis for a discussion: *Are stickers a good idea?*

Doctrinal content

2C: The Word became flesh for us in order to save us by reconciling us with God, who 'loved us and sent his Son to be the expiation for our sins'; 'the Father has sent his Son as the Saviour of the world' (*CCC* 457). The Church following the apostles teaches that Christ died for all men without exception: 'There is not, never has been, and never will be a single human being for whom Christ did not suffer'. (*CCC* 605)

Foundations in Year 7

Students should:

◆ show understanding of the difference between needs and wants

◆ understand that the New Testament proclaims Jesus as the Saviour

◆ understand how the liturgies of Holy Week celebrate the death and resurrection of Jesus.

Links to curriculum directory – KS3

The work in this section relates to the following aspects of the *RECD*. They are revisited and deepened throughout *Icons*. The learning outcomes for this section present the *RECD* for classroom use:

◆ human response to God's call to a covenant relationship and how this involves blessing, grace, struggle and weakness; – that Scripture and Tradition reveal God's love, mercy and forgiveness, which meet human faithfulness and sinfulness; (p. 17 – creation)

◆ the mission of Jesus as revealed in the New Testament with particular reference to his priestly, prophetic and kingly roles; – as priest, prophet and king Jesus proclaims the kingdom of God; (p. 22 – apostolic)

◆ the Church's vocation to have special care for the poor and oppressed; the Church's role as witness in society; – in the Church Christ's mission continues; – the Church's pastoral role: to be a revelation of God's love and forgiveness, the teacher and servant of the People of God. (p. 22 – mission)

For reflection

Question: At the name of Jesus … ?

Jesus was killed by those who thought they were saved already.

(Source unknown)

Consider this,
That in the course of justice none of us
Should see salvation; we do pray for mercy,
And that same prayer doth teach us all to render
The deeds of mercy.

(William Shakespeare, *The Merchant of Venice*, Act IV: 1)

By his first work He gave me to myself; and by the next He gave himself to me. And when He gave Himself, He gave me back myself that I had lost.

(Bernard of Clairvaux)

Catholic teaching

Jesus scandalised the Pharisees by eating with tax collectors and sinners as familiarly as with themselves. Against those among them 'who trusted in themselves that they were righteous and despised others' Jesus affirmed, 'I have not come to call the righteous, but sinners to repentance.' He went further by proclaiming before the Pharisees that, since sin is universal, those who pretend not to need salvation are blind to themselves.

Jesus gave scandal above all when he identified his merciful conduct toward sinners with God's own attitude toward them. He went so far as to hint that by sharing the table of sinners he was admitting them to the messianic banquet. But it was most especially by forgiving sins that Jesus placed the religious authorities of Israel on the horns of a dilemma. Were they not entitled to demand in consternation, 'Who can forgive sins but God alone?' By forgiving sins Jesus either is blaspheming as a man who made himself God's equal, or is speaking the truth and his person really does make present and reveal God's name. (*CCC* 588–9)

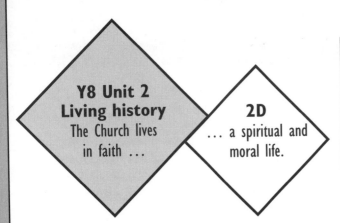

**Y8 Unit 2
Living history**
The Church lives
in faith ...

2D
... a spiritual and
moral life.

Summary of key learning

Sin is evidence of the **struggle between good and evil**. The Church recognises in the Genesis stories that sin is part of human life. No one can commit a sin by accident. **Conscience** guides and helps a person first to **judge what is right and wrong** and then **to make a decision** about what to do.

Teaching and learning process: *learning outcomes*

By the end of this section of work, students should:
◆ appreciate and recognise evidence of the spiritual and moral nature of the human person
◆ be introduced to the Church's teaching on the origin of sin
◆ know and understand Christian teaching about the role of conscience.

At each stage, select activities to fulfil the learning outcomes.

Research

Students will have the opportunity to investigate and reflect upon:
◆ how judgements and choices may be evidence of what people value
◆ evidence of common spiritual and moral values in school, family, society, the global community.

Revelation

Students will have the opportunity to learn about and reflect upon:
◆ how the Church interprets the Genesis presentation of the origin of sin
◆ the Church's teaching about what conscience is and the part it plays in human development
◆ how conscience is formed and developed, and the Catholic tradition of examination of conscience.

Response

Students will evaluate and reflect upon their learning. They will be given opportunities to make connections between their own experience and Revelation. They will:
◆ be able to evaluate to what extent people's values are reflected in their words and actions
◆ be able to explain how Genesis presents sin and the Church's teaching
◆ show knowledge and understanding of the Church's teaching about conscience
◆ show knowledge and understanding of the Catholic tradition of examination of conscience and its importance for Christian development.

Research

◆ *Where will it end?* (p. 57): explores the intrinsic worth of each human person. 'Worth-ship' (Anglo-Saxon) 'Worship', originally meant the quality of being valuable or worthy. Links to Y7, 3A, 'made in the image of God' and Y8, 1C, called to a unique vocation.
◆ *Extension* (p. 57): mission statement. Link to work in Y7, 1B.

Revelation

◆ **Diagnostic assessment**: *Check your learning* (p. 58): recalls Y8, 1C.
◆ *From good to evil* (p. 58): introduces the Genesis account of the fall. The figurative language focuses on the disruption of the relationship of the man and woman with God and with one another. From this flows evil, pain and suffering. The Catechism teaches that only in the knowledge of God's plan for humanity can we grasp that sin is an abuse of the freedom that God gives to created persons so that they are capable of loving him and loving one another. (*CCC* 387) It insists that this story can only be grasped in the light of the death and resurrection of Jesus Christ. (*CCC* 388) Symbolism of Genesis story, see *How to read the account of the fall* (*CCC* 390 and 396ff).
◆ *What's behind it all?* (p. 59): develops this Catechism teaching through New Testament examples. Jesus called people to the kingdom of God, the right relationship which he, as Son, reveals. The disputes over the details of keeping law show how far from its spirit the Pharisees and others had moved.
◆ **Formative assessment 1**: *Classwork* (p. 59).
◆ *Sin* (p. 60): deepens previous learning. Link to Y7, 2D. Jesus' parable of conversion is the prodigal son, who was loved, forgiven and restored to life in his Father's house.
◆ *Conscience* (p. 61): focus on objective and informed power to judge that flows from the right relationship with God (*CCC, In Brief*, p. 399). *Copymaster 12: Teacher's notes on Conscience*.
◆ **Formative assessment 2**: *Homework* (p. 61).
◆ **Elsewhere in *Icons***: the commandments as gift, light and guide, Y9, 1A.

Response: *Links (p. 62)*

◆ reflect deeper: *Pause for thought*
◆ literacy: *Key words*
◆ **Summative assessment**: *Test*
◆ question and go deeper: *Challenge*
◆ faith expressed in prayer: *Faith alive*

Tips for teachers

Resources

The Way Home (Veritas Productions) video, a parable of love

For teachers:
Moral Problems – What does a Christian do? Michael Pennock (Ave Maria Press)

Spiritual and moral links

Objective morality means accepting a 'higher authority' than the individual.

Additional activities

◆ Make an audit of one school day to identify choices made. Agree a scale for grading them, for example, from 'common/everyday' to 'seriously right or wrong'.
◆ Create a visual wall of images to show contrasts between good and evil.
◆ Explore other Genesis imagery of sin and conscience, e.g., Cain and Abel, Babel. (*Genesis* 4: 1–15; 11: 1–9)

Doctrinal content

2D: Conscience enables one to assume responsibility for the acts performed. The verdict of the judgement of conscience remains a pledge of hope and mercy. In attesting to the fault committed, it calls to mind the forgiveness that must be asked, the good that must still be practised, and the virtue that must be constantly cultivated with the grace of God. (*CCC* 1781)

Foundations in Year 7

Students should:

◆ appreciate the spiritual nature of the human person and the place of prayer in human life and faith
◆ know and understand Christian teaching about the importance of prayer and the significance of the 'Our Father' for Christians
◆ know and understand some of the ways Scripture and Tradition describe the role of the Holy Spirit in the life and work of the Church.

Links to curriculum directory – KS3

The work in this section relates to the following aspects of the *RECD*. They are revisited and deepened throughout *Icons*. The learning outcomes for this section present the *RECD* for classroom use:

◆ the Church's understanding of the story of the fall as related in Genesis and its consequences for human nature; – human nature is divided and subject to temptation; – Jesus is God's forgiveness and mercy; (p. 38 – dignity of the human person)
◆ the formation and cost of conscience, and consequences of misinformed or unformed conscience; opportunities for the exercise of freedom and responsibility in family life, the local church and society: at local, national and global levels; – the value the Church places on freedom, responsibility and conscience. (p. 38 – freedom, responsibility and conscience)

For reflection

Question: What do I believe about holiness? About sin?

Advice of a senior devil: It does not matter how small the sins are provided that their cumulative effect is to edge the man away from the light and out into nothing. Murder is no better than cards, if cards can do the trick. Indeed, the safest road to hell is the gradual one – the gentle slope, soft under foot, without sudden turnings, without signposts.

(C. S. Lewis, *The Screwtape Letters*)

The greatest of faults, I should say, is to be conscious of none.
(Thomas Carlyle)

Really to sin you have to be serious about it.
(Ibsen, *Peer Gynt*)

It is true that sin is the cause of all this pain; but all shall be well, and all shall be well, and all manner of thing shall be well.
(Julian of Norwich)

Catholic teaching

God created man in his image and established him in his friendship. A spiritual creature, man can live this friendship only in free submission to God. The prohibition against eating 'of the tree of the knowledge of good and evil' spells this out: 'for in the day that you eat of it, you shall die.' The 'tree of the knowledge of good and evil' symbolically evokes the insurmountable limits that man, being a creature, must freely recognise and respect with trust. Man is dependent on his Creator, and subject to the laws of creation and to the moral norms that govern the use of freedom. (*CCC* 396)

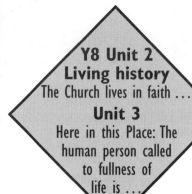

Y8 Unit 2
Living history
The Church lives in faith ...
Unit 3
Here in this Place: The human person called to fullness of life is ...

2/3E
... seeking unity and communion.

Summary of key learning
• •
Sunday worship shows the **unity, diversity and division** among Christian Churches. Jesus prayed that his followers would be one as he and his Father are one. The **Week of Prayer for Christian Unity** is one way of working for the unity for which Jesus prayed.

Teaching and learning process: *learning outcomes*

By the end of this section of work, students should:
◆ be able to identify unity and division in human life
◆ know and appreciate diversity and division among the Christian Churches in England and Wales
◆ know and understand Catholic teaching about ecumenism
◆ know about the Week of Prayer for Christian Unity.

Research
Students will have the opportunity to investigate and reflect upon:
◆ some of the benefits of being 'at one' in class, at school, at home, in organisations
◆ some of the pain that comes from division in class, at school, at home, in organisations
◆ the ways in which unity can be fostered and division overcome.

Revelation
Students will have the opportunity to learn about and reflect upon:
◆ the Church's teaching about diversity and division in the Church today, locally and nationally in England and Wales
◆ Catholic teaching about ecumenism
◆ the Week of Prayer for Christian Unity.

Response
Students will evaluate and reflect upon their learning. They will be given opportunities to make connections between their own experience and Revelation. They will:
◆ be able to identify and suggest ways of promoting unity and resolving division
◆ be able to recognise and describe the diversity and division among Christians
◆ demonstrate knowledge and understanding of Catholic teaching about ecumenism and the Week of Prayer for Christian Unity.

At each stage, select activities to fulfil the learning outcomes.

Research
◆ Illustrations (p. 63): explore unity of purpose.
◆ *Words we use* and *Pause for thought* (p. 63): explore concept of diversity.
◆ *Copymaster 13: Building up* and *Copymaster 14: Knocking down.*

Revelation
◆ **Diagnostic assessment**: *Check your learning* (p. 63). Work in Y7, 3C focused on naming different groups of Christians. Look for awareness of diversity and unity. Ecumenism is to do with other Christian Churches.
◆ *Project: The churches in our neighbourhood* (p. 64): creates context for work on Sunday worship.
◆ *Come worship the Lord* (pp. 64–65): introduces Anglican, Baptist and Quaker worship; local alternatives may offer links and scope.
◆ **Formative assessment 1**: *Classwork* (p. 65).
◆ *May they all be one* (p. 66): provides a context for Christian unity; focus on Jesus' prayer; historical background. Diversity is God's gift. Unity matters because the Church is witness to the loving communion of the Trinity. Unity in diversity is the challenge and hope for the Church (*CCC* 819–822). Division is falling short of the Church's vocation. It presents a different kind of challenge.
◆ *The sadness of division* (p. 67). The Word of God, the teaching of the apostles, the sacraments, the care of bishops united with the Bishop of Rome are Christ's gifts to his Church. The Catholic Church preserves all these gifts. Some Christian denominations have lost one or other of them. Some set an example of how to value better these gifts of the Lord, for example, the Protestant churches' example of how to appreciate the beauty of the Scriptures. Within the Catholic Church there is a multiplicity of peoples and cultures. 'Holding a rightful place in the communion of the Church there are also particular Churches that retain their own traditions'. (*CCC* 814) *Group task* (p. 67).
◆ *Hope for unity* (pp. 67–68): responses to the call to work for unity (a) Churches together in England and Wales (*CTE*); (b) the Week of Prayer for Christian Unity.
◆ **Formative assessment 2**: *Homework* (p. 68).
◆ **Elsewhere in *Icons***: key events that led to church division in England and Wales, Y9, 1B.

Response: *Links (p. 69)*
◆ creative response: *Design a symbol for Christian Unity*
◆ reflect and apply: *Pause for thought*
◆ literacy: *Key words*
◆ **Summative assessment**: *Test*
◆ question deeper: *Challenge*
◆ faith in the words of prayer: *Faith alive*
◆ opportunity for extended discussion/writing: *Another step*

Tips for teachers

Resources

Christians in Britain Today, D. Cush, Carol Miles, M. Styliandes (Hodder and Stoughton)

For teachers:
That All May Be One. Catholic Reflections on Christian Unity, E. Faladeau SSS (Paulist Press)

Spiritual and moral links

Recognising and understanding differences leads to tolerance and respect.

Additional activities

◆ Arrange for groups to visit at least two different Christian churches and prepare reports for the class or year group. Focus on similarities and differences.
◆ Invite a member of clergy from a Christian church of another denomination, or a panel of clergy, to participate in a question and answer session.
◆ Develop local history work from Y8, 1B. Choose one local Anglican church and research the phases of its Catholic and Anglican history.

Doctrinal content

2/3E: The Church is one: she acknowledges one Lord, confesses one faith, is born of one Baptism, forms only one Body, is given life by the one Spirit, for the sake of one hope (cf. Eph. 4:3–5), at whose fulfilment all divisions will be overcome. (*CCC* 866) 'The Church knows that she is joined in many ways to the baptised who are honoured by the name of Christian, but do not profess the Catholic faith in its entirety or have not preserved unity or communion under the successor of Peter'. (*CCC* 838) Desire to recover the unity of all Christians is a gift of Christ and a call of the Holy Spirit through conversion of heart and prayer in common. (cf. *CCC* 820, 821)

Foundations in Year 7

Students should:
◆ appreciate the demands of relationships for building community
◆ know and understand that the first Christians began to build community in response to Jesus' call
◆ know that there are different Christian Churches in England and Wales
◆ understand and appreciate the vital part forgiveness and reconciliation can play in change
◆ know and understand Christian teaching about the importance of prayer.

Links to curriculum directory – KS3

The work in this section relates to the following aspects of the *RECD*. They are revisited and deepened throughout *Icons*. The learning outcomes for this section present the *RECD* for classroom use:
◆ human response to God's call to a covenant relationship and how this involves blessing, grace, struggle and weakness; the human vocation to seek communion; – Scripture and Tradition reveal God's love, mercy and forgiveness which meet human faithfulness and sinfulness; (p. 17 – creation)
◆ the Church's role as witness in society; – the Church's pastoral role: to be a revelation of God's love and forgiveness, the teacher and servant of the People of God; (p. 22 – mission)
◆ the variety of prayer forms and their significance in Catholic life and history; – prayer as God's gift; variety of approaches to prayer and settings for prayer. (p. 31 – prayer)

For reflection

Question: If I pray for ecumenism how might I work for it?

Even where there is a difference in calling and some quite profound differences in belief, there may still be sharing. Christian partners do not have to be identical. Sharing can itself add a dimension to combined activity. The criterion we follow in responding to a call for joint action, or for the 'double act' at a meeting or religious service is 'Where one plus one can add up to more than two'.

(Archbishop Derek Worlock, Bishop David Sheppard, *Better Together*)

In order to be united we must love one another, to love one another we must know one another, to know one another we must meet one another.

Journalist: What is ecumenism? Liverpool docker: I suppose it's those two bishops sticking up for our jobs.

Catholic teaching

There can be no ecumenism worthy of the name without interior conversion. For it is from newness of attitudes of mind, from self-denial and unstinted love that desires for unity take their rise and develop in a mature way. We should therefore pray to the Holy Spirit for the grace of genuine self-denial, humble and gentle in the service of others (*Decree on Ecumenism*, 8).

Certain things are required in order to respond adequately to this call: a permanent renewal of the church in greater fidelity to her vocation; conversion of heart as the faithful try to live holier lives according to the gospel; prayer in common, spiritual ecumenism; fraternal knowledge of each other; ecumenical formation of the faithful and especially of priests; dialogue among theologians and meetings among Christians of different churches and communities; collaboration among Christians in various areas of service to mankind. (*CCC* 821)

Other Faiths
This is a flexible section. The RE Department will decide each year where it will be included.

Judaism
... significance of the Passover celebration for Jewish faith.

Summary of key learning

In every generation the Jewish people make **the Exodus experience** their own through the **Passover** celebration.

Teaching and learning process: *learning outcomes*

By the end of this section of work, students should:
◆ have an appreciation of the story of the Jewish community in Britain
◆ know and understand the significance of the Passover celebration.

At each stage, select activities to fulfil the learning outcomes.

Research

Students will have the opportunity to investigate and reflect upon:
◆ some aspects of the history of the Jews in Britain
◆ Jewish communities in Britain.

Research

◆ **Diagnostic assessment**: *Check your learning* (p. 70): assesses prior learning.
◆ *Jews in Britain* (p. 70): focuses on key moments in the Jewish story in Britain.
◆ *Extension* (p. 70): follow up with deeper historical focus or relate to present.

Revelation

Students will have the opportunity to learn about and reflect upon:
◆ the significance of Passover
◆ the Seder meal
◆ the Haggadah, retelling the story of deliverance and freedom.

Revelation

◆ Links to Y8, 2A and the study of Exodus. N.B. The Jewish faith, unlike other non-Christian religions, is already a response to God's revelation in the Old Covenant. To the Jews 'belong the sonship, the glory, the covenants, the giving of the law, the worship, and the promises; to them belong the patriarchs, and of their race, according to the flesh, is the Christ'; for the gifts and call of God are irrevocable. (*CCC* 839)
◆ *The Festival of Freedom* (pp. 71–73): introduces *Pesach* and *Seder* meal; explores symbolic food and symbolic actions (telling the story); introduces the *Haggadah*; key element – in every generation people must make their own the exodus experience (p. 71): *Copymaster 15: The Seder Table.*
◆ **Formative assessment 2**: *Homework* (p. 71).
◆ **Formative assessment 1**: *Classwork* (p. 73).
◆ **Elsewhere in** *Icons*: the flexible Other Faiths unit in Y9 focuses on the naming of God in Islam.

Response

Students will evaluate and reflect upon their learning. They will be given opportunities to make connections between their own experience and Revelation. They will:
◆ demonstrate knowledge and understanding of Jewish communities in Britain
◆ be able to describe key moments in the Passover celebration
◆ be able to explain the importance of the Passover celebration for Jewish believers.

Response: *Links (p. 72)*

◆ apply learning: *Pause for thought*
◆ opportunity for research/extended writing: *Another step*
◆ **Summative assessment**: *Test*
◆ literacy: *Key words*
◆ question and think deeper: *Challenge*
◆ faith in words of prayer: *Faith alive*

Tips for teachers

Resources

Judaism for today, Angela Wood (*Religion for Today series*, OUP, 1997)

For teachers:
A Passover Haggadah, ed. by Herbert Bronstein (Penguin Books, 1987)

Spiritual and moral links

Freedom and hope of freedom are essential for the human person.

Additional activities

◆ A visit to a modern synagogue. This could complement the work on the background and culture in which Jesus grew up, Y8, 1A.

◆ Invite a Jewish family to describe their *Pesach* celebrations, or contact a local synagogue or local centre for a Jewish speaker, or watch a video.

◆ Research other festivals celebrated by the Jewish community in Britain today.

Doctrinal content

Judaism: The Jewish faith, unlike other non-Christian religions, is already a response to God's revelation in the Old Covenant. To the Jews 'belong the sonship, the glory, the covenants, the giving of the law, the worship, and the promises; to them belong the patriarchs, and of their race, according to the flesh, is the Christ'; 'for the gifts and the call of God are irrevocable'. (*CCC* 839)

Foundations in Year 7

Students should:

◆ appreciate the power of symbol in human life

◆ be able to explain why it is important to respect other faiths

◆ show appreciation of the common search for God.

Links to curriculum directory – KS3

The work in this section relates to the following aspects of the *RECD*. They are revisited and deepened throughout *Icons*. The learning outcomes for this section present the *RECD* for classroom use:

◆ the Church's teaching about the need to recognise 'seeds of the Word' in other faith communities; – that community life is valued and lived in all faith communities; – of the Church's teaching about respect for the life and belief of other faith communities; (p. 22 – mission)

◆ traditions and way of life of other faith communities in England and Wales; – of community values of other faith communities in England and Wales. (p. 38 – the human community)

For reflection

Who belongs to the Catholic Church? The whole human race is called to this Catholic unity of the People of God ... and to it, in different ways, belong or are ordered: the Catholic faithful, others who believe in Christ, and finally all humanity, called by God's grace to salvation. (*CCC* 836)

A Jew at heart remains a Jew, his country is his soul.

(Eileen Duggan)

Catholic teaching

The relationship of the Church with the Jewish People

When she delves into her own mystery, the Church, the People of God in the New Covenant, discovers her link with the Jewish People, 'the first to hear the Word of God'. The Jewish faith, unlike other non-Christian religions, is already a response to God's revelation in the Old Covenant. To the Jews 'belong the sonship, the glory, the covenants, the giving of the law, the worship, and the promises; to them belong the patriarchs, and of their race, according to the flesh, is the Christ'; 'for the gifts and the call of God are irrevocable' (*CCC* 839).

... and when one considers the future, God's People of the Old Covenant and the new People of God tend towards similar goals: expectation of the coming (or the return) of the Messiah. But one awaits the return of the Messiah who died and rose from the dead and is recognised as Lord and Son of God; the other awaits the coming of a Messiah, whose features remain hidden till the end of time; and the latter waiting is accompanied by the drama of not knowing or of misunderstanding Christ Jesus. (*CCC* 840)

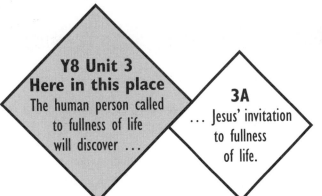

**Y8 Unit 3
Here in this place**
The human person called
to fullness of life
will discover ...

3A
... Jesus' invitation
to fullness
of life.

Summary of key learning

Human dignity is based on **God's invitation** to
each person to be **holy**, sharing God's life.
Response to this invitation can often be costly.
Jesus challenges his followers to work so that
all can have **fullness of life**.

Teaching and learning process: *learning outcomes*

By the end of this section of work, students should:

◆ appreciate the wonder and mystery of being human
◆ know more about and understand Jesus' invitation to 'fullness of life'.

At each stage, select activities to fulfil the learning outcomes.

Research

Students will have the opportunity
to investigate and reflect upon:

◆ the wonder and beauty of some
human virtues (strengths) and
qualities – openness to truth and
beauty, freedom, sense of moral
goodness, longing for
happiness, curiosity, love of
justice
◆ what develops these virtues and
qualities and what weakens
them.

Revelation

Students will have the opportunity
to learn about and reflect upon:

◆ the gospel invitation to 'fullness
of life'
◆ how Christian belief in human
dignity is lived out.

Response

Students will evaluate and reflect
upon their learning. They will be
given opportunities to make
connections between their own
experience and Revelation. They
will:

◆ demonstrate understanding and
appreciation of the richness of
human qualities and virtues
◆ demonstrate knowledge,
understanding and appreciation
of the gospel call to 'fullness of
life'
◆ have opportunities to reflect on
the challenge to Christians to live
the call to fullness of life.

Research

◆ *A place for everyone* (pp. 75–76): examines strengths and qualities
that make human beings the apex of God's creation; focus begins
through parents' hopes for a child; spiritual nature of human
persons demonstrated in imagination, human curiosity, capacity
for awe and wonder, ability to give self in relationships, powers of
perseverance. N.B. For human, moral and theological virtues see
CCC 1804–1832.
◆ **Diagnostic assessment**: *Check your learning* (p. 76): look for
knowledge and understanding of God as Creator and God's call
to human persons.

Revelation

◆ *Life to the full* (p. 77): Jesus' invitation to fullness of life and the
relationship with God this offers is explored through the gospel
story of the rich young man. Focus on opportunity, possibilities,
challenge and response. An opportunity to explore 'happiness'
(passing) and 'blessing' (endless); a foundation for work on
'Kingdom of God' which follows in Y8, 3C and in Y9.
◆ **Formative assessment 2**: *Homework* (p. 77).
◆ *Words we use* (p. 78): key vocabulary and imagery for exploring
the mystery of 'the kingdom'. Explore grain of wheat image as
key to Christian faith and to the mystery of the cross. By Christ's
death and resurrection, humanity is set free *from* sin and death
and free *for* life that is eternal. Link back to Y8, 3A, the Easter
message and to Y7, 3A, Celebrating Life – the Eucharist is the
pledge of eternal life and glory. (*CCC* 1402–1405 and 1419)
◆ *The cost of discipleship* (p. 79): explores the paradox of the cross –
the new life that comes through letting go. Alternative people
might be chosen to reflect local history (e.g. school patron saint)
or current events.
◆ **Formative assessment 1**: *Classwork* (pp. 78–79).
◆ **Elsewhere in *Icons***: holiness of life as mark of Church, the
communion of saints Y8, 3D; all are called to share Jesus' life
and sacrifice, Y9, 2D; how Jesus challenges disciples to seek
fullness of life for all and the common good, Y9, 3A.

Response: *Links (p. 80)*

◆ think deeper: *Pause for thought*
◆ literacy: *Key words*
◆ a gospel challenge: *Challenge*
◆ words of prayer inspired by and supporting faith: *Faith alive*
◆ **Summative assessment**: *Test*

Tips for teachers

Resources

Youth 2000 (St Paul Multimedia) video
Number One; Stranger; In the Bin (Scripture Union Productions) video

For teachers:
A Spirituality of Wholeness, a new look at grace, Bill Huebsch (Twenty-Third Publications, 1988)

Spiritual and moral links

Self-esteem which grows from awareness of human dignity as God-given is one of the most important factors in living a full life.

Additional activities

◆ Research hopes and dreams of 'forever' in popular songs, for example, 'I want to live forever'. What do these dreams of happiness say about being human?

◆ Research groups and organisations in the locality that work to help people to have real quality of life. For example, support for mothers and toddlers, senior citizens. How are the gifts and dignity of helpers and helped used and recognised? Decide on how to present your findings.

Doctrinal content

3A: 'All Christians in any state or walk of life are called to the fullness of Christian life and to the perfection of charity.' All are called to holiness: 'Be perfect, as your heavenly Father is perfect'. (*CCC* 2013) Spiritual progress tends towards ever more intimate union with Christ. (*CCC* 2014)

Foundations in Year 7

Students should:

◆ understand and appreciate the importance of relationships for community

◆ know and understand Jesus' call to discipleship

◆ appreciate Catholic belief that the Eucharist is central to the Church's life and teaching.

Links to curriculum directory – KS3

The work in this section relates to the following aspects of the *RECD*. They are revisited and deepened throughout *Icons*. The learning outcomes for this section present the *RECD* for classroom use:

◆ humanity as created by God; awareness of the transcendent and the holy and of the Presence of God in self, others and the world; – the Church's teaching about human life, dignity and vocation; (p. 17 – creation)

◆ the life and ministry of Jesus, his teaching, parables and miracles; – Jesus is God become man so that human beings might share the life of God; (p.17 – Jesus Christ)

◆ the Church's vocation to have special care for the poor and oppressed; the Church's role as witness in society; – in the Church, Christ's mission continues; the Church's pastoral role: to be a revelation of God's love and forgiveness, the teacher and servant of the People of God. (p. 22 – mission)

For reflection

Question: What moves me to wonder?

Stages of Faith

Interest
Acceptance
Awareness
Belonging
Questioning
Making Sense
Communicating Christ

Life begins at 75! According to Scripture, Abram was 75 when he heard and responded to God's call.

Everyone moved by the Spirit is a son of God. The Spirit you have received is not a spirit of slaves to bring fear into your life again; it is the Spirit of sons, and it makes us cry out 'Abba, Father'. The Spirit and our spirit bear united witness that we are children of God.

(Romans 8: 14–16)

Catholic teaching

It is only in the mystery of the Word incarnate that light is shed on the mystery of humankind. It is Christ, the last Adam, who fully discloses humankind to itself and unfolds its noble calling by revealing the mystery of the Father and the Father's love …

Christians are certainly subject to the need and the duty to struggle against evil through many tribulations and to suffer death; but they share in the paschal mystery and are configured to the death of Christ, and so are strengthened in the hope of attaining to the resurrection. This applies not only to Christians but to all people of good will in whose hearts grace is secretly at work. Since Christ died for everyone, and since the ultimate calling of each of us comes from God and is therefore a universal one, we are obliged to hold that the Holy Spirit offers everyone the possibility of sharing in this paschal mystery in a manner known to God.

(*Pastoral Constitution on the Church in the World of Today*, 22)

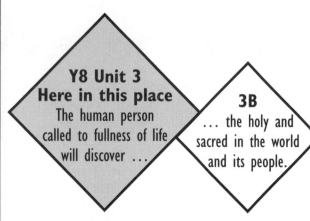

Y8 Unit 3
Here in this place
The human person called to fullness of life will discover ...

3B
... the holy and sacred in the world and its people.

Summary of key learning

Creation reflects the beauty and goodness of God the **Creator**. Human beings are called to co-operate with God by respecting and caring for the gifts of creation.

Teaching and learning process: *learning outcomes*

By the end of this section of work, students should:
- appreciate that reverence for creation is a human instinct
- have a deeper appreciation of Christian belief that creation reveals God and that human beings are called to be co-workers with God.

At each stage, select activities to fulfil the learning outcomes.

Research

Students will have the opportunity to investigate and reflect upon:
- evidence that people show respect and reverence for creation
- evidence of some of the ways in which people abuse creation.

Research

- *A task worthy of God* (p. 81): use the story or video to introduce this example of creative care for the earth.
- *Classwork* (p. 81): respect for the world begins 'at home'; local initiatives may provide material for research into how individuals and groups work for the environment.

Revelation

Students will have the opportunity to learn about and reflect upon:
- how Scripture expresses reverence for creation as designed and created by God and entrusted to human beings
- how Christian art, liturgy and prayer present God as Creator and creation as God's gift.

Revelation

- *Co-workers with God* (p. 82): develops understanding of creation as God's work; reinforces/introduces concept of 'stewardship' of creation; links to work on Genesis and humanity as 'crown' of creation, Y7, 3A and Y8, 2D.
- *Getting the message* (p. 82): assesses opportunities for stewardship.
- *The Christian heritage* and *God ever present* (pp. 83–84): opportunities for research; a local retreat centre may have resources for exploring the spirituality of God's creation.
- **Formative assessment 2**: *Homework* (p. 85).
- *Covenant with creation* (p. 85): two texts: Psalm 104 (Jewish text, BC) and Grail text (20th century AD): Deepens understanding of interdependence of human persons and creation; of creation as good and as a gift, an inheritance destined for and entrusted to humanity. (*CCC* 299) At the same time the universe 'did not spring complete from the hands of the Creator, but is "in a state of journey" toward an ultimate perfection and in this human beings are co-workers with God. (*CCC* 302)
- *Copymasters 16* and *17*: Additional material.
- **Formative assessment 1**: *Classwork* (p. 85).
- **Elsewhere in *Icons***: the sacramentality of life is developed further in Y9, 1D and 2C; personal holiness is explored again in Y8, 3D and Y9, 2A.

Response

Students will evaluate and reflect upon their learning. They will be given opportunities to make connections between their own experience and Revelation. They will:
- be able to evaluate the evidence for respect for, and abuse of, creation
- demonstrate knowledge, understanding and appreciation of how Scripture and Tradition teach about God the Creator and creation as God's gift
- be able to evaluate the extent to which Christian teaching affects and challenges people to care for the earth.

Response: *Links (p. 86)*

- literacy: *Key words*
- **Summative assessment**: *Test*
- think deeper: *Pause for thought*
- question: *Challenge*
- faith in words of prayer: *Faith alive*
- apply learning: *Another step*

Tips for teachers

Resources
Song of Creation (CAFOD, 2000) cassette
Anthology for the Earth, ed. Judy Allen (Walker Books, 1997) models for graphics

For teachers:
The Greening of the Church, Sean McDonagh (Geoffrey Chapman, 1990)
A World Made Whole, Esther de Waal (Fount, 1991) rediscovering the Celtic vision

Spiritual and moral links
Care for the earth is part of the privilege and responsibility of being co-workers with God.

Additional activities
◆ Use *Pause for thought* (p. 81) to engage students in a project to collect materials for reuse. Ask students: *How can you make this a whole school issue and a collaborative project? What cross-curricular skills and expertise might be involved?*
◆ Write an account for a local newspaper of your campaign or write a letter to the editor about one aspect of the local natural environment that needs attention.
◆ Compose words and music for a modern day psalm in praise of creation.

Doctrinal content
3B: Creation has its own goodness and proper perfection, but it did not spring forth complete from the hands of the Creator. The universe was created 'in a state of journeying' (*in statu viae*) toward an ultimate perfection yet to be attained, to which God has destined it. We call 'divine providence' the disposition by which God guides his creation toward this perfection. (*CCC* 302) To human beings God gives the power of freely sharing in his providence by entrusting them with the responsibility of 'subduing the earth' and having dominion over it. (*CCC* 307)

Foundations in Year 7
Students should:
◆ know and understand the Christian belief that the gift of life is the beginning of a loving relationship – covenant– with God and that human beings have a unique place in creation
◆ appreciate the power of symbol in human life
◆ know and understand the significance of the sacrament of the Eucharist for Catholics.

Links to curriculum directory – KS3
The work in this section relates to the following aspects of the *RECD*. They are revisited and deepened throughout *Icons*. The learning outcomes for this section present the *RECD* for classroom use:
◆ awareness of the transcendent and the holy and of the Presence of God in self, others and the world; – Scripture records from the beginning God's blessing in creation, God's call to stewardship, the problem of human sinfulness and good and evil; (p. 17 – creation)
◆ opportunities for the exercise of freedom and responsibility in family life, the local church and society at local, national and global levels; – the value the Church places on freedom, responsibility and conscience; (p. 38 – freedom, responsibility, conscience)
◆ the universal value of some signs and symbols; – the place of universal signs and symbols in the life of the Church. (p. 30 – sacraments)

For reflection

Question: What, above all, do I value in creation?

The world's present and future depend on the safeguarding of creation, because of the endless interdependence between human beings and their environment. Placing human wellbeing at the centre of concern for the environment is actually the surest way of safeguarding creation; this in fact stimulates the responsibility of the individual with regard to natural resources and their judicious use.

(John Paul II, *World Day of Peace 1999*)

Beauty will save the world. Art reveals the glory – reveals the abstract. All is sacrament.
(Fedor Dostoevsky)

Catholic teaching

Icons

In the 8th century a controversy about the honour paid to icons led the Church to reflect on the sacredness of created things and matter. The theological debate was resolved in the light of faith in the Incarnation. St John of Damascus said 'I shall not cease to honour matter for it was through matter that my salvation came to pass'. (*In Defence of Holy Icons*)

God wills the interdependence of creatures. The sun and the moon, the cedar and the little flower, the eagle and the sparrow: the spectacle of their countless diversities and inequalities tells us that no creature is self-sufficient. Creatures exist only in dependence on each other, to complete each other, in the service of each other.

The order and harmony of the created world results from the diversity of beings and from the relationships which exist among them … The beauty of creation reflects the infinite beauty of the Creator and ought to inspire the respect and submission of man's intellect and will. (*CCC* 340–1)

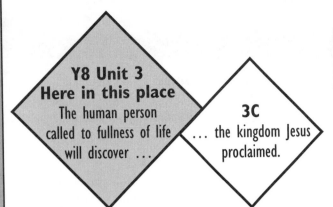

Y8 Unit 3
Here in this place
The human person
called to fullness of life
will discover …

3C
… the kingdom Jesus
proclaimed.

Summary of key learning

Jesus taught about the **Kingdom of God** through **parables**. He challenges people to think about 'kingdom' in a new way. The parables **inspire** hopes and dreams.

Teaching and learning process: learning outcomes

By the end of this section of work, students should:
◆ have reflected upon the kind of world they would like to help create
◆ know some gospel imagery about the Kingdom of God and appreciate its significance.

Research

Students will have the opportunity to investigate and reflect upon:
◆ their hopes and dreams of creating a better world
◆ evidence that hopes and dreams inspire people to 'break boundaries', to overcome fears and doubts, and work to build a better world.

Revelation

Students will have the opportunity to learn about and reflect upon:
◆ how Jesus proclaimed the Kingdom of God in parables and what a parable is
◆ how the parables of the Kingdom inspire hopes and dreams: seed, net, banquet, sower, pearl, treasure, tree.

Response

Students will evaluate and reflect upon their learning. They will be given opportunities to make connections between their own experience and Revelation. They will:
◆ have had the opportunity to express their hopes and dreams for a better world
◆ have reflected on some of the ways in which people 'break boundaries'
◆ demonstrate knowledge and understanding of the gospel parables of the Kingdom of God
◆ be able to explain why Jesus used parables and why they still inspire Christians today.

At each stage, select activities to fulfil the learning outcomes.

Research

◆ *Does everyone have a dream?* (p. 87): starting point: Martin Luther King's speech – a dream of hope and freedom; opportunities for creative work and use of multimedia skills.
◆ **Diagnostic assessment**: (p. 87): *Check your learning*: offers a link to Revelation, which will explore the hope and freedom of the Kingdom of God that Jesus proclaims.

Revelation

◆ The focus in this section is on the gospel imagery of the Kingdom of God. Students will learn that a parable is a literary form and a teaching method that Jesus used to shock his listeners into attention. (*CCC* 546) It will be important to make links back to the different religious groups (Y8, 1A) to appreciate how and why the parables would have shocked.
◆ *A greater hope* (pp. 88–90): themes to look for include: the kingdom is for all, it belongs to the poor and lowly – that means those who accept it with humble hearts; sinners are invited to the table of the kingdom. (cf. *CCC* 543–545) Notice to whom Jesus gives a higher profile. The kingdom is 'within', it is about a relationship with God.
◆ **Formative assessment 1**: *Classwork* (pp. 88–89). N. B. Section B: Luke 14:15–24 is a more challenging parable; the messianic banquet is a sign of the joy to come (cf. Isaiah 25:6). Jesus' listeners would have been familiar with this concept, so, his apparent welcome to sinners would have shocked some listeners. Section C offers an opportunity for exploring the nature of people's relationship with God. Links to Y8, 2D and 3A should challenge awareness of the cost of the kingdom and the 'darkness that needs God's light'.
◆ *The Parable of the Sower* (p. 90): provides an opportunity for a creative exercise in interpreting the parable for today.
◆ **Formative assessment 2**: *Homework* (p. 90).
◆ **Elsewhere in *Icons***: the Christian vision of the kingdom 'on earth and in heaven', Y9, 3D.

Response: *Links (p. 91)*

◆ think deeper: *Pause for thought*
◆ **Summative assessment**: *Test*
◆ literacy: *Key words*
◆ question and think deeper: *Challenge*
◆ faith inspires prayer: *Faith alive*
◆ extended application of learning for discussion/writing: *Another step*

Tips for teachers

Resources

In the Footsteps of Christ (St Paul Multimedia Productions) video no. 4

For teachers:
The Kingdom of God is like… Thomas Keating OCSO (Crossroad Publishing, 1997)

Spiritual and moral links

Encouraging people to have a 'dream' or a 'vision' is leading them beyond themselves.

Additional activities

◆ For extended writing, or a year group debate, think about the statement, *The Kingdom of God is here and now and not yet.*

◆ Use a selection of newspapers and magazines to identify people for whom a vision of the kingdom might offer hope, and why.

◆ Discuss how Jesus' vision of the kingdom affirms and challenges the hopes and dreams for the better world students identified at the beginning of this section. Plan and run a reflection time (an hour or half a day) using your findings.

Doctrinal content

3C: Jesus' invitation to enter his kingdom comes in the form of parables, a characteristic feature of his teaching. Through his parables he invites people to the feast of the kingdom, but he also asks for a radical choice: to gain the kingdom one must give everything. Words are not enough, deeds are required. The parables are like mirrors … Jesus and the presence of the kingdom in this world are secretly at the heart of the parables. (*CCC* 546)

Foundations in Year 7

Students should:

◆ appreciate the demands of relationships for building community

◆ know and understand that the first Christians began to build community in response to Jesus' call

◆ have an appreciation of how Christians witness to the resurrection in daily life.

Links to curriculum directory – KS3

The work in this section relates to the following aspects of the *RECD*. They are revisited and deepened throughout *Icons*. The learning outcomes for this section present the *RECD* for classroom use:

◆ passages from Scripture which speak of God; – how Scripture names God; (p. 17 – trinity)

◆ humanity as created by God; – the Church's teaching about human life, dignity and vocation; (p. 17 – creation)

◆ Jesus' imagery of the 'kingdom of God'; – the Church's understanding of its nature and role in the world; (p. 22 – church)

◆ the mission of Jesus as revealed in the New Testament with particular reference to his priestly, prophetic and kingly roles; – as priest, prophet and king, Jesus proclaims the kingdom of God. (p. 22 – apostolic)

For reflection

Question: Where do I find the kingdom on earth as it is in heaven?

The kingdom invites Christians to be 'actors' not 'reactors'.

Jesus' conviction that the 'kingdom' would come, that humanity could and would be totally liberated, would have been impossible without his belief in God.

(Albert Nolan, *Jesus Before Christianity*)

Our call to the Kingdom, which each of us must face, is this: I cannot say my 'yes' of love to God without saying my 'yes' of love to you. In the Kingdom of God I am never less than an individual, but I am never only an individual. I am always a member of a group called by God to a response of love, which must include the whole group or it is literally unacceptable to God.

(John Powell SJ, *The Christian Vision*)

Catholic teaching

Jesus' invitation to enter his kingdom comes in the form of parables, a characteristic feature of his teaching. Through his parables he invites people to the feast of the kingdom, but he also asks for a radical choice: to gain the kingdom, one must give everything. Words are not enough, deeds are required. The parables are like mirrors for us: will we be hard soil or good earth for the word? What use have we made of the talents we have received? Jesus and the presence of the kingdom in this world are secretly at the heart of the parables. One must enter the kingdom, that is, become a disciple of Christ, in order to 'know the secrets of the kingdom of heaven'. For those who stay 'outside', everything remains enigmatic. (*CCC* 546)

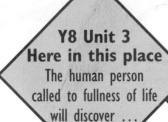

Y8 Unit 3
Here in this place
The human person
called to fullness of life
will discover ...

3D
... the holiness,
diversity and strength
of the communion
of saints.

Summary of key learning

The Church is the **communion of saints**. The Church **canonises** some men and women and names them in the **calendar of saints**. Saints are **witnesses**, in every walk of life, to the life and mission of Christ in the Church.

Teaching and learning process: *learning outcomes*

By the end of this section of work, students should:
◆ understand and appreciate the significance of being known by name
◆ understand what it means to say that the Church is 'the communion of saints'
◆ know and appreciate how the Church celebrates the holiness and example of men and women through the ages.

At each stage, select activities to fulfil the learning outcomes.

Research

Students will have the opportunity to investigate and reflect upon:
◆ why it is important to be called by name
◆ how they got their names and how they feel about them
◆ how names reflect times and history, and how family, famous people and fashions influence naming.

Revelation

Students will have the opportunity to learn about and reflect upon:
◆ patron saints
◆ the great variety of saints honoured in Catholic Tradition
◆ Catholic belief that the Church is 'the communion of saints': canonised, uncanonised, 'dead' and living, saints by popular acclaim
◆ the power of saints to be witnesses in the life and work of the church.

Response

Students will evaluate and reflect upon their learning. They will be given opportunities to make connections between their own experience and Revelation. They will:
◆ demonstrate an appreciation of the importance of being known by name
◆ know about the calendar of saints and be able to identify some patron saints
◆ be able to explain the significance of saints in the life of the church.

Research

◆ *My name is ...* (p. 92): introduces the idea of linking a name with a significant person
◆ *Find out what your name means* (p. 92): encourages an awareness of names. The Cardinal Hume story provides a way into a discussion about the importance of names, how we should be sensitive to them, and so on.

Revelation

◆ *Christian names* (p. 93): make the link between Christian names and baptism.
◆ **Diagnostic assessment**: *Check your learning* (p. 93): assesses prior learning.
◆ *All saints!* (p. 93): introduces/develops how the Church names and celebrates saints.
◆ *Saints alive* (p. 94): explores how the Church honours and recognises saints through canonisation.
◆ **Formative assessment 2**: *Homework* (p. 94).
◆ *The Communion of Saints* (p. 94): the communion of saints is the Church. (*CCC* 946) Link to anointing (anointing makes holy) at Baptism and Confirmation – Y7, 1D and Y8, 1D; also to the Church, disciples, who live in communion with Jesus, Y7, 1A and Y8, 2A.
◆ *Patron saints* (p. 95): Baptism and Confirmation are a call to witness; the power of example: opportunity for work on national and local saints.
◆ **Formative assessment 1**: *Classwork* (p. 95).
◆ **Elsewhere in *Icons***: Students will explore further the concept of the Church as the kingdom of God in terms of gospel people and gospel values if they next do 2/3E. If already completed, make links.

Response: *Links (p. 96)*

◆ extend and apply learning: *Another step*
◆ literacy: *Key words*
◆ **Summative assessment**: *Test*
◆ imagine: *Pause for thought*
◆ question: *Challenge*
◆ faith that inspires prayer: *Faith alive*

Resources

Patron Saints, Michael Freze, SFO (Our Sunday Visitor Publications, 1992)

Today We Celebrate, Gerard MacGinty OSB (Collins, 1985)

For teachers:

Revised Calendar of Saints for England and Wales, 2000 (available from Liturgy Office, 39 Eccleston Square, London SW1V 1BX)

Spiritual and moral links

Wholeness and holiness are two sides of the same coin.

Additional activities

◆ Research family names passed down through generations. Ask students: *Why does this happen?*

◆ Introduce some time (10 minutes each week) to read about the lives of saints.

◆ Have a class/year notice board and display the saints' days from the liturgical calendar. Suggest that students undertake to choose one saint each and provide a thumbnail biography (three sentences).

◆ Prepare an assembly on one recently canonised saint.

Doctrinal content

3D: The communion of saints *is* the Church (*CCC* 946). The term 'communion of saints' has two closely linked meanings: communion 'in holy things', and 'among holy people'. (*CCC* 948) 'Exactly as Christian communion among our fellow pilgrims brings us closer to Christ, so our communion with the saints joins us to Christ, from whom as from its fountain and head issues all grace, and the life of the People of God itself'. (*CCC* 957)

Foundations in Year 7

Students should:

◆ understand how self-esteem, self-knowledge and respect contribute to the growth and development of each person

◆ appreciate that the creative energy and imagination of human beings is evidence of their spiritual nature

◆ know and understand Baptism is the beginning of Christian discipleship

◆ know how Christians recognise and name the creative power of the Holy Spirit in the world.

Links to curriculum directory – KS3

The work in this section relates to the following aspects of the *RECD*. They are revisited and deepened throughout *Icons*. The learning outcomes for this section present the *RECD* for classroom use:

◆ human response to God's call to a covenant relationship and how this involves blessing, grace, struggle and weakness (original sin); the human vocation to seek communion; – that Scripture and Tradition reveal God's love, mercy and forgiveness, which meet human faithfulness and sinfulness; (p. 17 – creation)

◆ the Church's understanding of vocation, exemplified in Mary, lived by local and national saints and communities; – the Church's understanding and teaching about vocation and the need for a personal response to God; (p. 22 – one and holy)

◆ the Church's role as witness in society; – the Church's pastoral role: to be a revelation of God's love and forgiveness, the teacher and servant of the People of God. (p. 22 – mission)

For reflection

Question: Why should I become a saint?

The only difference between the Saint and the Sinner is that every saint has a past and every sinner has a future.

(Oscar Wilde, *A Woman of No Importance*)

Can one be a saint if God does not exist?

(Camus, *The Plague*)

It is possible to keep laws with almost military precision. But virtues are neither exact nor codified. They are essentially embodied. They live not in rulebooks but in persons, not in the abstract but in history. We do not learn virtues as we learn rules, nor grow in them as we become more punctilious. It is in narratives, in stories, that we perceive them; as the Old Testament epics embodies the ideals of Judaism, as the lives of the saints set before us Christian holiness in all its variety. As we identify, enter into stories and feel our way through them, we are able to share, at first vicariously, but then in reality, in the qualities they represent.

(Kevin Nichols, *Refracting the Light*)

Catholic teaching

The Church is held, as a matter of faith, to be unfailingly holy. This is because Christ, the Son of God, who with the Father and the Spirit is hailed as 'alone holy', loved the Church as his Bride, giving himself up for her so as to sanctify her; he joined her to himself as his body and endowed her with the gift of the Holy Spirit for the glory of God. The Church then, is 'the holy People of God', and her members are called 'saints'. (*CCC* 823)

The communion of saints is the Church.

The term 'communion of saints' therefore has two closely linked meanings: communion 'in holy things' (*sancta*), and 'among holy persons' (*sancti*). *Sancta sanctis!* ('God's holy gifts for God's holy people') is proclaimed by the celebrant in most Eastern liturgies during the elevation of the holy Gifts before the distribution of communion. (*CCC* 946, 948)

In the footsteps of Jesus

Make a pilgrim's map for a five-day visit.

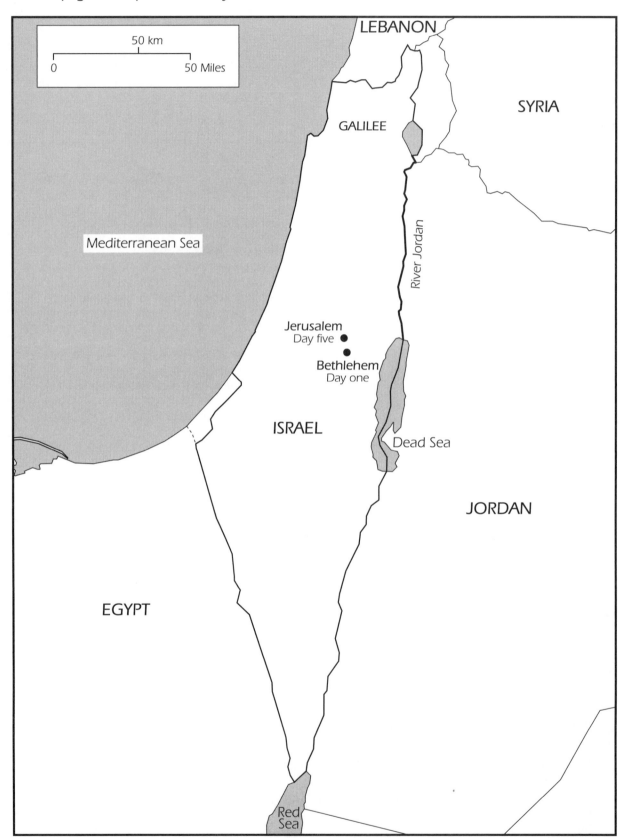

Prehistory

Legend has it that **Joseph of Arimathea** came to Britain and settled at **Glastonbury**. He was the man who got permission to bury the body of Jesus. Stories say that he brought with him the cup (grail) used at the Last Supper. From these stories grew the legends of King Arthur, the Round Table and the quest for the Holy Grail.

There is no historical evidence for who were the first Christians in Britain.

Roman Britain (50–450)

Among the Roman settlers and soldiers were Christians. Evidence of these Christians can be found at various places throughout Britain. At **Caerleon**, the Roman fort outside Newport, Gwent, Christian graffiti can be found. Remains of one of the earliest churches were found at **Silchester**, Berkshire. This church follows the pattern of a Roman basilica. A mosaic with a Christian theme can be seen at **Lullingston** Roman Villa, Kent.

In the persecution of Diocletian, **Julius** and **Aaron** are named among those martyred at Caerleon. They are celebrated as protomartyrs of Britain together with **St Alban**.

Bede's story of St Alban (*Copymaster 4*) is full of signs and miracles. St Alban's shrine was an early place of pilgrimage.

313AD ...... Emperor Constantine issued the Edict of Tolerance and Christians could worship openly.

Evidence of Christianity among native Britons is limited, but British bishops were present at the Church Councils at Arles (**314AD**), Sardica (**374AD**) and Rimini (**359AD**).

Anglo-Saxon Britain (450–1066)

The Benedictine scholar Dom David Knowles described this period in terms of 'Faith, Love and Loyalty'.

In the North:

Missionaries from Ireland brought Christianity to Scotland, the North of England, Wales and Cornwall.

565AD ...... **Columba** established the monastic tradition on the island of Iona (*Bede Book III, Ch IV*).

635AD ...... **King Oswald** of Northumbria invited Bishop Aidan to preach the Gospel (*Bede Book III, Ch. III*). **Aidan** established a monastery on **Lindisfarne**. The kingdom of **Northumbria** played a key role in the Church in Britain. Monks and bishops (for example, **Benet Biscop** and Wilfrid) made the pilgrimage to Rome and brought back books. The library at **Jarrow** was famous and **Bede** is its best-known scholar.

Saints of the North:

Cuthbert, Hilda of Whitby, Wilfrid of Ripon and Hexham, John of Beverley, Bede.

In the South:

597AD ...... Missionaries from Rome, sent by **Pope Gregory the Great**, arrived in Kent. **Augustine** became the first Archbishop of Canterbury. **King Ethlebert** of Kent welcomed him and gave him land to build a monastery because **Queen Bertha**, a princess from Gaul, was a Christian.

Paulinus, a monk of Canterbury, was a missionary to the North East before becoming Bishop of Rochester.

Saints of the South:

Etheldreda of Ely, Erconwald of London, Ethelburga of Barking, Mildred of Thanet.

In Wales:

Gildas (born c.500AD) wrote a book, which he called *The Ruin of Britain*. He castigates the British kings for their infidelity to the Christian heritage of Rome.

St Patrick, a Roman Briton, taught the Irish that because they were Christians, they should also be Romans.

Wales and England developed as distinct entities in the struggles of the Britons to maintain the heritage of Rome – of which Christianity was the central pillar.

Monasticism came early to Wales. The first outstanding figures were **St Cadoc** and **St Illtud**. The latter is remembered as the greatest Christian teacher among the Britons. In the sixth century, the monastic movement began the re-evangelisation of the Christian Britons in Cornwall and Wales, and along the Western seaboard. The greatest name associated with this movement is **St David** (died 589). In those early times, the links between the monasteries of Wales and Ireland were close and seafaring was the easiest form of travel.

Saints of Wales:

David (Dewi) Pembrokeshire.

Illtud, abbot of the monastery of Llantwit in Glamorgan.

Samson, abbot of Caldey Island who became a missionary to Cornwall, Brittany and the Channel Islands.

Links with the Universal Church

There were good links between the Church in Britain and Gaul (France) and with Rome. The many churches dedicated to **St Peter** in England are a sign of the devotion to the saint, for which the Church in Britain became noted. (Peter's Pence, a collection for the Papacy, originated in Britain.) Pilgrimage *ad limina* – to the threshold of Peter's tomb – became a sign of faith and loyalty. Today, bishops of every country pay regular *ad limina* visits to Rome.

There were cultural differences between the Celtic and Roman traditions. For example, the diocese was a Roman form of organisation, while for most Celtic bishops, their monastery was their base. The two traditions calculated the date of Easter in different ways. This became a practical and political issue.

664AD ...... the **Synod of Whitby** brought together followers of both traditions. The Roman way of calculating the date of Easter was accepted. Until this time Roman and Celtic traditions celebrated Easter on different days (*Bede, Book III Ch. XXV*). The Welsh Church did not adopt the Roman way of dating until 768.

Dark times

The growth of Christianity in Britain was severely tested by the Viking and Danish invasions.

793AD ...... Lindisfarne was destroyed by pagan raiders.

794AD ...... Jarrow, with its library, was burned. Throughout England and Wales the learning and art of the monasteries was destroyed. For three hundred years Vikings in the North and Danes in the South fought and raided.

Alfred, King of Wessex (871–c. 901) rallied the English. He fought the Danes, but made peace when he could. He then did his best to restore the learning that was lost with the destruction of monasteries and the years of war and uncertainty. **Alphege**, archbishop of Canterbury, was martyred at Greenwich (1006). The Danish invaders pelted him with the bones of their feast and finished him off with an axe. On 28 December 1065 **King Edward the Confessor** attended the consecration of the abbey church at Westminster. Eight days later he died.

Medieval Britain (1066–1500)

Writing of these times, Dom David Knowles identifies as key features, 'Law, Discipline and Authority'. These can be traced in both Church and State.

William the Conqueror invaded Britain with the approval of the Pope. The Norman drive to centralise power, however, often led to clashes with the Church. The king granted land to the Bishops as 'spiritual lords' and barons as 'secular lords'. In return they swore fealty to the king, paid taxes and supplied men for his army. Successive Archbishops of Canterbury played an important part in the history of this time.

Anselm, Archbishop of Canterbury (1093–1109), was a scholar and writer. William II (Rufus) refused to let him go to Rome to receive his pallium. He accused Anselm of sending substandard soldiers for the king's war in Wales, and exiled him. Later, Henry I also exiled Anselm.

Thomas a Becket was Henry II's chancellor. They quarrelled over the right to judge clerics. Thomas was murdered in his cathedral at Canterbury. Henry did public penance for his part in the events that led up to Thomas' murder.

Stephen Langton, Archbishop of Canterbury, is the first name among the witnesses to the Magna Carta signed by King John.

During these centuries the Church was also developing a more central organisation. The Roman Curia was developed. Cardinals gained new influence. The authority of the Pope extended through a system of papal legates and judge delegates. This extended the rule of law and discipline in the Church, but it was also open to abuse. The *Code of Canon Law* was formulated and English lawyers and churchmen made a significant contribution to this.

One way of demonstrating power was in buildings. Many of the great castles, cathedrals and abbeys date from this time. **Monastic schools** offered education, but only a few went to school. The first colleges of Oxford and Cambridge were founded. Only men could be scholars and most were clerics, or planned to take holy orders. There was no national welfare and it was the **monasteries** that provided care for the poor and the sick. **Places of pilgrimage** became important and churches or monasteries associated with them made money from the pilgrims. Examples of these include: the shrine of St Thomas a Becket at Canterbury, Walsingham in Norfolk, St Cuthbert's tomb in Durham and, in Wales, the shrines of St David and St Winifride.

Source texts from Bede – St Alban

Bede's *Ecclesiastical History of the English People, Book I Ch. VII*

[AD 305] Alban, who, though still a pagan, at the time when heathen emperors were issuing savage edicts against the Christians, gave hospitality to a priest who was in flight from his persecutors. Alban noticed that he devoted himself day and night to continual prayer and vigil, and suddenly he himself received the gift of divine grace and began to imitate the example of his faith and piety. Gradually, instructed and encouraged by him in the way of salvation, he abandoned the darkness of idolatry and became a whole-hearted Christian.

After this priest had been staying as his guest for several days, it came to the ears of the wicked ruler that one who confessed the Christian faith – but who was not yet destined for martyrdom – was hiding at Alban's home. He at once ordered his soldiers to make a thorough search for him there. When they arrived

at the martyr's humble dwelling, Alban at once offered himself to the soldiers in place of his guest and teacher, wearing the clothing, that is to say the cloak, worn by the priest. He was bound and taken before a judge.

When the judge realised that he could not be broken by torture nor turned back from the worship of the Christian religion, he ordered him to be beheaded. As he was being taken to his death, he came to a fast-flowing river, which separated the city wall and the arena where he was to be executed; and he saw there a large crowd of men and women of every age and rank, who without doubt were summoned by divine inspiration to escort the most blessed confessor and martyr. They filled the bridge over the river itself in such numbers that he could hardly have crossed that evening.

So Alban, whose burning desire was to come quickly to his martyrdom, approached the torrent, and as he lifted his eyes to Heaven, suddenly the riverbed became dry and he saw that the water had receded and made a way for him to walk.

[At this the executioner refused to kill him. Alban climbed a nearby hill accompanied by the crowd. Bede describes the hill in detail as 'a fit place to be hallowed by the blood of a blessed martyr'.]

On top of the hill Alban asked God for a gift of water, and at once a perpetual spring gushed up at his feet, channelled into a stream, to prove to them all that even the torrent had rendered service to the martyr.

And so the brave martyr was beheaded on that spot and received the crown of life that God has promised to those that love Him. But the man who laid unholy hands upon his holy neck was not permitted to gloat over his body: his eyes dropped to the ground together with the blessed martyr's head.

Anglo-Saxon Chronicle

286AD. In this year St Alban, the martyr, suffered martyrdom.

(Laud Chronicle; the Parker Chronicle gives the date as 283.)

Bede's *Ecclesiastical History of the English People, Book IV Ch. XXIV*

In the monastery of Whitby was a brother specially favoured by the grace of God in that he used to compose songs on religious and devotional themes. Whatever of the Holy Scriptures he learned through interpreters he would render in a short time in his own, that is, the English tongue, in a most melodious and moving poetic diction.

[The brother was Caedmon, sometimes called the first English poet. He was a herdsman at the monastery. Like many others at the time he could not read, but what embarrassed him more, was that he could not sing. When the feasting turned to singing he would leave the warmth of the hall for the cold dark stable where he slept.]

In his dream someone stood beside him, who greeted him and called him by his name, 'Caedmon' he said, 'sing something to me.' He replied, 'I don't know how to sing that is why I left the feast and came out here, because I could not sing.' Again the one who spoke to him said, 'Yet you must sing me something.' 'What should I sing?' he asked. He said, 'Sing of the beginning of creation.' Hearing this reply, Caedmon at once began to sing, in praise of God the Creator, verses, which he had never heard before. When he arose, he remembered everything that he had sung in his sleep, and later added to it more verses in the same manner, singing God's praise in fitting style.

[The Abbess of the monastery was Hilda. She tested Caedmon's gift and discovered that if a passage of the Bible or the teaching of the Church was explained to him he could turn it into skilful poetry. She encouraged him to join the monastery as a monk so that he could know the riches of the Bible and saw that he had good teachers.]

Caedmon stored in his memory everything that he could learn by listening to them, like a clean animal chewing the cud, and turned it into the sweetest poetry, and by his more melodious utterance, made his teachers become in turn his audience.

This is the opening line of Caedmon's poem in Anglo-Saxon:

Nu schulon herigan   *heofonrices Weard,*

This is a translation of his poem into modern English:

How fitting that we worship   Heaven's guardian,
The power of the Maker   the wisdom that is his
The Father's works: when of his wonders
God the Lord   made the beginning!
First he fashioned   for the earth's children
Heaven as a roof,   the Holy Workman!
Then the earth   Heaven's Guardian
the Eternal God,   he adorned
for mankind,   the Almighty Lord.

1. What do you learn from the two texts from Bede (Copymasters 4 and 5) about:
    a   the writer and the Christian community to which he belonged?
    b   the people whose stories he tells?

2. What do you learn about the work of historians who want to write about this period of history? What other sources might they consult?

The bishops asks all who are about to be confirmed to renew the profession of faith made in Baptism.

To each question the candidates reply: I do.

- ◆ Do you reject Satan and all his works and all his empty promises?
- ◆ Do you believe in God the Father Almighty, creator of heaven and earth?
- ◆ Do you believe in Jesus Christ, his only Son, our Lord,
    who was born of the Virgin Mary,
    was crucified, died and was buried,
    rose from the dead, and is now seated at the right hand of the Father?
- ◆ Do you believe in the Holy Spirit, the Lord, the giver of life,
    who came upon the apostles at Pentecost
    and today is given to you sacramentally in confirmation?
- ◆ Do you believe in the holy catholic Church,
    the communion of saints, the forgiveness of sins,
    the resurrection of the body, and life everlasting?

Bishop: This is our faith. This is the faith of the Church. We are proud to profess it in Christ Jesus our Lord.

All: Amen.

Prayer at the laying on of hands:

In Baptism, God our Father gave the
new birth of eternal life
to his chosen sons and daughters.
Let us pray to our Father,
that he will pour out the Holy Spirit
to strengthen them with his gifts
and to anoint them to be more like
Christ the Son of God.

The bishop and priest present extend their hands over all who are to be confirmed.

The bishop prays:

All-powerful God, Father of our Lord Jesus Christ,
by water and the Holy Spirit
you freed your sons and daughters from sin
and gave them new life.
Send your Holy Spirit upon them
to be their helper and guide.
Give them the spirit of wisdom and understanding,
the spirit of right judgement and courage,
the spirit of knowledge and reverence.
Fill them with the spirit of wonder and awe in your presence.
We ask this through Christ our Lord.

Is your birthday anything like this?

Birthdays are a celebration of the past and a way of looking forward to the next part of our lives.

1. Read or act out this story.

> Scene: Joshua's bedroom. Enter Mum and Alice (his younger sister) carrying a birthday cake with candles.

> **Mum and Alice:** *(singing) Happy birthday to you, Happy birthday to you, Happy birthday dear Joshua, happy birthday to you!*

> **Joshua:** *(embarrassed and a bit grumpy) Thanks, but I'm a teenager now and a bit old for you to sing to me. Can you get out now so I can get dressed?*

> **Mum:** *Well hurry up! Your Gran's come round to see you and Alice is dying to help you open your presents.*

> Later. Down in the kitchen.

> **Gran:** *(as Joshua walks in) Many happy returns! Where's a kiss for your old Gran?*

> **Grandad:** *(to Mum as Joshua kisses his Gran) It doesn't seem like 13 years ago does it, love?*

> **Mum:** *No. I remember it as if it was yesterday – this gorgeous little bundle in my arms.*

> **Joshua:** *Oh Mum! Stop going on!*

> **Gran:** *Come on. Open your cards. (She hands him a card.) Happy birthday dear, and many more of them.*

> **Alice:** *Can I help you open your presents?*

2. Is your birthday anything like this?

3. What does Gran mean by 'many happy returns'?

4. Why do you think Mum remembers so clearly something that happened so long ago?

5. What hopes do you think Grandad would have had for Joshua when he first saw him 13 years ago?

6. How do you think Joshua's grandparents feel today on his thirteenth birthday?

Make a note of your answers to share with the class.

1. Design an image of the Church as the People of God.
   Here are some key points to remember.

The People of God grow through:

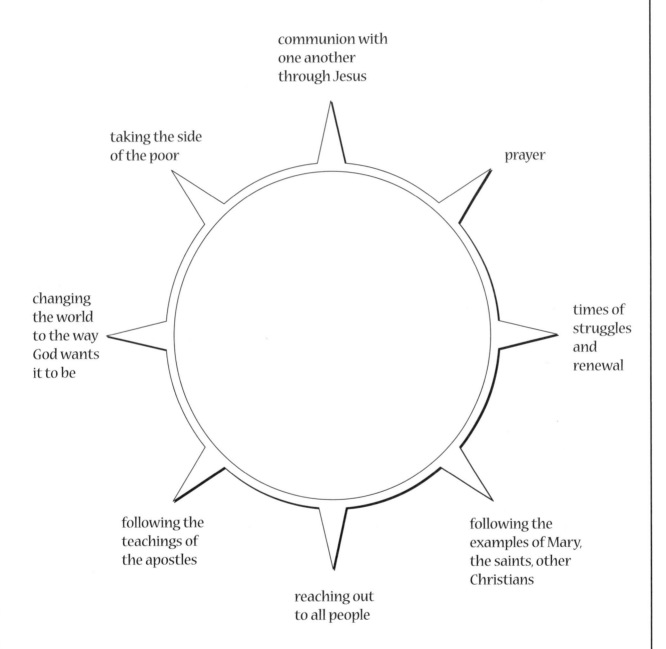

communion with
one another
through Jesus

taking the side
of the poor

prayer

changing
the world
to the way
God wants
it to be

times of
struggles
and
renewal

following the
teachings of
the apostles

following the
examples of Mary,
the saints, other
Christians

reaching out
to all people

2. Write a short reflection on the image you have designed.

Prayers for the Sacrament of Reconciliation

Alternatives for the Invitation to Trust

May God, who has enlightened every heart, help you to know your sins and trust in his mercy.

May the Lord Jesus welcome you. He came to call sinners, not the just. Have confidence in him. May the grace of the Holy Spirit fill your heart with light, that you may confess your sins with loving trust and come to know that God is merciful.

May the Lord be in your heart and help you to confess your sins with true sorrow.

Let us listen to the Word of God:

God's words to Israel are words for all people
How can I give you up?
How can I abandon you?
My heart will not let me do it!
My love for you is too strong.
I will not punish you in my anger.
For I am God. I, the Holy One, am with you.
I will not come to you in anger. *(Hosea 11: 8, 9)*

The Lord is compassion and love, slow to anger and rich in mercy.
For as the heavens are high above the earth so strong is his love for those who fear him.
As far as the east is from the west so far does he remove our sins. *(Psalm 103: 8,11–12)*

Prayers of Sorrow

Lord Jesus, you chose to be called the friend of sinners.
By your saving death and resurrection free me from my sins.
May your peace take root in my heart
and bring forth a harvest of love, holiness and truth.

O my God, because you are so good,
I am very sorry that I have sinned against you,
and with the help of your grace
I will not sin again.

Praise and Thanksgiving

May the passion of our Lord Jesus Christ,
the intercession of the Blessed Virgin Mary and of all the saints,
whatever good you do and suffering you endure,
heal your sins,
help you to grow in holiness,
and reward you with eternal life.
Go in peace.

Blessed are those whose sins have been forgiven,
whose evil deeds have been forgotten.
Rejoice in the Lord, and go in peace.

Take each of these situations.

A

Crowded sweet shop
One shop assistant
Lots of pushing and shoving
Young person with little money

B

Group of close friends
One boy/girl picked on
Take his/her bag or sports kit
Push a little, shove a little

1. Identify the 'pull' towards the good and the less good, the bad or even the evil.

2. Present your findings in role-play, illustrations or written dialogue.

3. Write about what ACTION a young Christian might take to help him or her to avoid getting into such a situation.

4. In what ways might the Sacrament of Reconciliation help Christians to cope with the tension between 'good' and 'evil'?

OR

   What have you learned from your work on the Sacrament of Reconciliation about the gifts God offers to help Christians in their struggle between 'good' and 'evil'?

5. A survey:
   Interview three people from different generations.
   Ask each for an example of how they felt this 'pull'.
   Share your findings with the class.
   Draw up and list your conclusions about human nature.

Prayers for the Sacrament of Anointing of the Sick within Mass

The Sacrament of the Anointing of the Sick can be celebrated for an individual at home, in hospital or as part of a celebration of the Eucharist.

Opening Prayer for the Sacrament of the Sick within Mass

We have come together to celebrate the sacraments of anointing and the Eucharist. Christ is always present when we gather in his name; today we welcome him especially as physician and healer. We pray that the sick may be restored to health by the gift of his mercy and made whole in his fullness.

Prayers of Intercession

Let us pray to God for our brothers and sisters and for all those who devote themselves to caring for them.

Bless *N.* and *N.* and fill them with new hope and strength: Lord have mercy.

R. *Lord have mercy.*

Relieve their pain: Lord have mercy.

R. *Lord have mercy.*

Sustain all the sick with your power: Lord have mercy.

R. *Lord have mercy.*

Assist all who care for the sick: Lord have mercy.

R. *Lord have mercy.*

Give life and health to our brothers and sisters on whom we lay our hands in your name: Lord have mercy.

R. *Lord have mercy.*

Prayer of Anointing

The priest anoints each sick person on the forehead saying:

Through this holy anointing may the Lord in his love and mercy
help you with the grace of the Holy Spirit.

Prayer after the Anointing

May the Lord who frees you from sin
Save you and raise you up.
Father in heaven,
through this holy anointing
grant our brothers and sisters comfort in their suffering.
When they are afraid, give them courage,
when afflicted, give them patience,
when dejected, afford them hope,
and when alone, assure them of the support
of your holy people
We ask this through Christ our Lord.
Amen

Extension

Look up these readings. Which would you choose for a mass with the sick, and why?

The Liturgy of the Word

Romans 8:26–27   Romans 8:31–35, 37–39.
Psalm 101:2–3   Psalm 102:1–4
Matthew 15:29–31   John 10:11–15

Teacher's notes on Conscience

Certain words which in common parlance are interchangeable need to be given precise definitions if necessary distinctions are to be drawn. So in this note:

GOOD / BAD describe the *objective reality* of conformity or non-conformity between my proposed act and **God's law**. (cf. *Veritas Splendor* 59)

CORRECT / INCORRECT describe conformity or non-conformity between *my judgement* and **that reality**. (*VS* 62)

RIGHT / WRONG describe conformity or non-conformity between *my decision* (about how to act) and **that judgement**. (*VS* 61)

My *judgement* about God's will with regard to the proposed act before me is informed by several sources. For example:

INSTINCT – my natural feelings. Many wrongly regard this element as the whole of conscience. But it is not to be despised: it is ever present, although very fallible.

CONSENSUS – what normal decent people think. Insofar as this represents an aggregate of 'instincts' it is more reliable than one instinct alone, but it is rather less accessible: 'What **do** normal decent people think?'

AUTHORITY – the declaration of a specialist. Even less accessible, because rarely seen as directed to my particular case in all its circumstances; but once established, it is the most secure of all contributions to my judgement. (*VS* 64)

My conscience is my JUDGEMENT, *all things considered,* **about how I should act.** It is an intellectual act, not susceptible of moral evaluation. It is correct or incorrect – not good or bad, not right or wrong – in the terms defined above.

It is theoretically quite separate from my subsequent **DECISION** about whether or not to conform my act to my judgement. That is a volitional act, morally right or morally wrong – not good or bad, not correct or incorrect – in the terms defined above.

In reality I tend to anticipate the consequences of my judgement, and try not to admit judgements which will lead to disagreeable decisions. Hence the confusion of these two processes which analytically deserve to be kept quite distinct.

So there are four possibilities with regard to a positive act:

1. My judgement is **correct** (I judge what is objectively good to be good, what is objectively bad to be bad) and I decide **to act in accordance** with my judgement (to do what I judge to be good).
    Then my action is objectively GOOD and morally RIGHT.

2. My judgement is **incorrect** (I judge good what is objectively bad…); I decide **to act in accordance** with my judgement (to do what I judge to be good).
    My action is objectively BAD, but morally RIGHT.

3. My judgement is **correct** (I judge good what is objectively good…); I decide **not to act in accordance** with my judgement. (I do what I judge to be bad.)
    My action is objectively BAD, and morally WRONG.

4. My judgement is **incorrect** (I judge good what is objectively bad…); I decide **not to act in accordance** with my judgement. (I do what I judge to be bad.)
    My action is objectively GOOD, but morally WRONG.

Since 1 and 2 are both 'morally right', one might ask whether making the 'correct' judgement is of any importance. The answer has to be 'Yes', since an incorrect judgement will otherwise lead an innocent person to self-damaging action. (*VS* 63)

On the bricks write words that name situations and attitudes that build unity and real divisions. Some ideas to get you started have been added.

FRIENDLINESS A CELEBRATION

A HELPING HAND WILLING TO FORGIVE

On the wrecker write words that name situations that break down unity and cause division.

Here are some ideas to get you started:

anger   **looking for revenge**   **unhappiness**   **disloyalty**

Three Matzah

The bread of affliction that our ancestors ate in haste when they fled from Egypt.

Shankbone of lamb

The paschal sacrifice offered by each family on the eve of the Passover.

Egg

This symbolises sacrifice and the Jewish people. It is said that just as the egg hardens when heated, so the Jewish will to survive becomes more resolute with persecution.

Maror

These bitter herbs recall the pain of slavery.

Haroset

Chopped apples and nuts are mixed with cinnamon and wine. This recalls the mortar for the building work which the Hebrews were forced to do.

Karpas

These are green herbs, usually parsley or celery. They are a symbol of spring and new life.

Bowl of salt water

This is for dipping karpas into. It recalls the tears of the slaves.

Four cups of wine

Wine is the symbol of joy and redemption. The four cups recall God's fourfold promise of freedom.

Cup of Elijah

This recalls the prophet who will announce the coming of the Messiah.

Read Genesis 1:26–30 and Luke 12:16–21 and then discuss:

1. What message do these passages from the Bible give about the way in which the earth and her people are to be treated?

2. How well do these modern pieces present attitudes to creation today?

The Pacific Women's Creed

We believe that Creation is a gift from God,
an expression of our Creator's goodness.
We believe that the resources of our lands and waters and air
are precious gifts from our Creator, to be used and looked after with loving care.
We believe that there is a rhythm to God's creation, like a drum beat.
When we lose the rhythm, or the drum is damaged, the music is out of tune.
We believe that as Christians, we are called to be peacemakers,
in order that our world and our communities, and each person may experience the
*   true peace which God promises.*
We believe this may sometimes mean 'disturbing the peace', as Jesus did for a
*   purpose – to restore the purpose of God.*
We believe that our Pacific ways are also a gift from God.
We are invited to use the values of our Pacific cultures to build societies of justice
*   and peace.*

In the end man destroyed the place called earth.
The earth had been lovely
Until man's spirit moved over the face of the earth and
    destroyed all things.
And man let there be darkness.
And the darkness seemed good to them
and they named it Security
and divided themselves into races and religions and
    classes.
And there was no morning or evening
the seventh day before that final day.

And man said: Let there be a strong government to
reign over us in our darkness;
let there be armies that kill one another,
let there be order and efficiency in our darkness,
let us hunt down and destroy all those who tell us the
    truth,
here and unto the ends of the earth
because we preserve our darkness.
And there was no evening or morning
the sixth day before that final day.

And man said: Let there be missiles and bombs
and there were gas chambers and ovens
to finish the task more efficiently
the fifth day before that final day.

And man said: Let there be drugs
and every kind of escape
because we must avoid the constant nagging of Reality
which gets in the way of our comfort,
the fourth day before the final day.

And man said: Let there be division among nations
so that we may know who our enemies are,
the third day before that final day.

And man finally said:
Let us make god in our own image and likeness,
not some other god who will compete with us.
A god that thinks as we think
who hates what we hate
and who kills as we kill
the second day before that final day.

On that last day
there was a great explosion on the face of the earth; fire
purged that once beautiful world,
and there was silence.
And the Lord God saw
what man had done,
and in the silence
that enveloped the earth's smoking ruins
God wept.

(Iglesias, Mexico City, 1987)

What to do

Read through this information.

Polluted air has few boundaries. It can pass across national frontiers; poison produced in one country can end up thousands of miles away.

Imagine that you are the editor of a newspaper. Make up a news headline for each of the facts below:

Scientists estimate that carbon dioxide is expected to raise average temperatures by three degrees Celsius

Over 18,000 of Sweden's 85,000 lakes are acidified

450,000 tonnes of lead are released into the atmosphere each year – half of this comes from car exhausts

A hole the size of the United States has appeared in the ozone layer over Antarctica. Scientists have little doubt that chloroflorocarbon (CFC) pollution is the prime cause.

One-fifth of the world's population – 1.1 billion people – breathe air that is unsafe according to international limits on pollution.

50% of trees in the Black Forest in West Germany have been destroyed by acid rain

References in the index are to topics found in the students' book

Index